CHINA BLUE 1984

CHINA BLUE 1984

WAY OFF THE BEATEN TRACK...

Rosalinda Ruiz Scarfuto

Forest Flaneur Publications

Contents

In Memory of Joan

A woman of great courage in her own quiet way.

Acknowledgements

I would like to thank my family and friends who have given me support in more ways than one to this project. In times of my long absences from extended escapades to foreign lands, they never forgot me and welcomed me home ready to listen to my stories. I never had enough time or energy to write it all down until now. This book began as a way to humor myself after losing the use of my right hand with a wrist injury. There were times when I could not even write my name with a pencil or type on a keyboard without fumbling in pain. However, reminiscing about comedic episodes from this unique travel diary, literally became an integral part of my recovery---both physically and emotionally. Even when I doubted, I could continue, my friends and family were cheering on the sidelines. Hence, I decided to finish for them.

I would also like to thank my writing mentor, Alice, who caringly nudged me in ways I wouldn't have been able to do by myself. Her questions, suggestions, techniques and expertise led me beyond my own expectations; how to weave my stories into a book. I must admit her patience and insights were quite timely, especially when I was at a difficult crossroads in my life. I am ever so grateful.

I would dearly like to thank my friend Jill, who pushed me out of the nest to travel and introduced me to her mother, Joan. I hope this book reveals the amazing qualities of Joan (my companion) on the road, under wildly unusual circumstances, in her most natural self---smiling and living life to its fullest!

Author's Introduction

This story began 40 years ago in Hong Kong when I was 24 and innocently careless, with a blank diary tucked away in my backpack along with my new Canon camera. Sifting through the stream of babble from those pages of my diary (that comes with excitement on the road) along with photos, I pieced together my hilarious journey in China in the ominous year of '1984'. Mind you, we had all been acquainted with G. Orwell's infamous novel 1984 in English literature class in the 1970's, marking my first introduction to science fiction. Nevertheless, my trip was the real deal and Orwell's 'Big Brother' concept was a bit on the event horizon at the edge of a black hole in an authoritative country like China at the time.

My sojourn in China was part of a longer five-year journey across the globe as a young backpacker, completed by age 27. This unique part of the story is set in Mainland China (People's Republic of China-PRC) and covered the entire country starting in the south, roaming as far north as inner Mongolia, east and west. I won't give you any more clues so you can follow along the trail with open eyes, relive the absurd obstacles and detours that make this tale even beyond most backpackers' experiences in 1984! In my case ignorance was bliss and a cocktail for mishaps. Luckily, I had a semi-rational companion, Joan, that kept me safe; she was an adventurous spirit with few limits, and her opinion was invaluable. In 1984 the mere fact was that China was not the mega powerful entity participating on the world market as it is today, and things were simpler back then; no one was in a hurry moving around on trains, buses, bicycles or planes. Their smiles were more apparent in a sea of BLUE mao suits (uniform attire inspired by Mao; cotton blue pants and blue shirt to match). Both men and women dressed alike, creating fewer distractions. This is a glimpse of a country on the precipice of becoming a superpower; albeit unimaginable from where I was sitting, listening to the slow bureaucratic wheels turning under a rickety train window in 1984. China's drastic transformation can be duly appreciated by indulging with me in these first-hand observations as the story unfolds, which may seem unbelievable in comparison to today's reality of ultra-modern China. Lest we forget, a country is made up of its people.   Truly the most valuable memories of this unforgettable sojourn were our interactions with the people. Believe it or not, we could not speak Chinese and yet we enjoyed experiences with various types of people along the way, mostly using our survival skills in pantomime, charades, smiles and, now and again, English. My intention here is twofold: share my memoirs and give an insight into the people that have many times been misunderstood as a group.

For historical purposes I should outline the basics. Hong Kong was still British controlled, on the verge of being turned over to China after a 99-year lease agreement (negotiation) from the 19th century wars. Taiwan, an island, was part of China until Chiang Kai-Shek as the leader of the Chinese Nationalists declared Taiwan not part of 'commu-nist' China, calling it the Republic of China (ROC). The two territories, Hong Kong and Taiwan, were supported by western allies to varying degrees carried over from earlier 20th century events. Britain had its own reasons to remain diplomatic with Mao, the People's Republic of China (PRC) since 1950 and not necessarily recognize Taiwan. France at first recognized Taiwan along with the United States, but in 1964 switched over to open diplomatic relations with Mao.

The United States remained firm not to recognize Mao as the leader of China for decades after 1949. Instead, Taiwan had been the official diplomatic representative of the Chinese government until a break in policy was announced by President Nixon, followed by a historic visit to meet Mao. No American citizen could step foot inside Mainland China before that famous handshake between President Nixon and Chairman Mao in 1972. I was reading Edgar Snow's book, *Red Star Over China* (famous for his interviews with Mao in clandestine territories) as I traveled around China. He was an American student journalist living in Peking before 1949. I gathered some basic historical concepts from his perspective that is helping me through a maze of political jockeying that converted China into a unique communist country without Stalin's support by the end of its revolution.

According to Snow, Japan had already invaded China by 1936 at the time Snow was writing his book and he claims western influences were supporting Japan. It had subsequently created an anticolonial sentiment for both Mao and Chiang Kai-Shek to take advantage of the situation in a combined effort to oust the Japanese from their homeland. However, these two Chinese leaders' political ties and concept of China's future, post-Japanese colonial rule, differed and eventually culminated in their rivalry. Therefore, by the time Japan was defeated in 1945, Mao and Chiang Kai-Shek were in two camps: nationalists and communists. Mao stood firm in his position having led the 'red' armies in defense of the 'people' to secure his position. The Japanese military was especially brutal on the borders of their colonial rule and the red armies were relentless in defending these border villages. Snow explains that Mao had become popular with land redistribution for the masses. Chiang Kai-Shek on the other hand appealed to the landowning classes and land redistribution had become unpopular owing to the loss of personal advantages. Chinese conflicts between these two camps resulted in Chiang Kai-Shek abandoning the mainland for Taiwan to escape defeat (imprisonment).

After Mao's victory in 1949 China closed its doors except for rare diplomatic meetings. With Chiang Kai-Shek as leader of the Taiwan territory, it became known as a rogue territory in the eyes of Mainland China; yet a recognized 'country' to some western ears. From Chiang Kai-Shek's perspective, one day reunification would put Taiwan at the center of Chinese people as the Republic of China (ROC) and defeat the People's Republic of China. When I first visited Taiwan in 1984 leaving Japan by boat on my way once again to Hong Kong, I was puzzled when I saw a video clip showing how Taiwan (a tiny island) would take over Mainland China. Highlight: In its national museum, Taiwan did house many of the Chinese art treasures that had been saved from the Cultural Revolution.

Without going into tedious policy detail over the next few decades, Hong Kong and Taiwan are not independent territories or separate countries; they are both linked culturally and politically to the Mainland Chinese belt. Before 1999 (return to sender China), British Hong Kong was a kind of hub for southeast Asian travelers. It was also a strange combination of East and West, and somehow comfortable for westerners; an oasis in the middle of Asia. How did I end up becoming a regular visitor in Hong Kong? Don't ask me why, but my first trip to Asia (Japan) went via Hong Kong. So, suddenly when I was landing in Hong Kong at midnight for the first time in 1982, it was when it dawned on me; my life would change forever. I just did not know exactly how it would play out. I suppose it's similar to my grandparents who had left Europe, I risked all to live out a daydream. It starts like this…

I was prompted to join a grad student friend, Susan, on a long motorcycle trip. She was finishing her PhD at the same time I was finishing my B.A. in a California academic setting and we both wanted a break before a 'real job'. It gave me motivation to finish my degree on time before traveling and not waste another year. I had changed my major shortly before this planned adventure and it required a double-down studying effort to finish at the same time. Unfortunately, Susan did not finish her PhD; understandably, given her research was molecular biology related to brain cells (pretty darn complicated)! Nevertheless, I was ready to travel after graduation and to be free! I was so excited about the idea of traveling, and it got lodged into my brain because it was the perfect excuse to avoid the inevitable assimilation into the 'real' world after graduation from university. My parents had saved diligently to provide a higher education for me; they were hoping I would meet a husband or at least get a decent job, but that was not the case.

By the time graduation time was rolling around, I was on my own; I did not even follow my graduating classmates. Some were off to backpack around Europe for cultural fun. My own immigrant family was fresh off the boat from the poverty stricken 'old country' (Spain and Italy). My grandparents on both sides had already sacrificed all to live out the "American Dream", determined to move the next generations forward. Europe in my family was not seen as an amusement trip for student hosteling and pub crawls, but rather a step backwards. New York was another popular destination for recent graduates to experience the cosmopolitan life of the East coast, or for west coast L.A. dwellers like me; not my choice either. My mom, having grown up in Brooklyn, always complained of the cold and the despair she felt there. Her parents had advanced forward to sunny California seeking a better life!

Basically, California is the end of the road of the North American continent, meaning there is not much else except an ambiguous blur in the distance of the South Pacific. I had often sat on the beach, daydreaming of Asia, where the sinking sun could be seen on the horizon of the Pacific, the vast divide between East and West. Six months before graduation, I was nonchalantly sitting on the beach with Joan's daughter Jill and her roommate, who offered me a job in Japan to help out at a summer camp. I was not completely convinced, but with a little nudging from Jill, I applied for my first passport. Why not?

That was two years ago, after a string of unexpected experiences such as landing a job in the middle of the Japanese rice fields, signing a contract and changing my visa status from an ordinary tourist to a student studying Japanese. Not to mention my opium delirium experience that set me on a new course during a gastritis bout when I was coming back from my visa trip to South Korea. It was just supposed to be a routine trip to secure a visa for my new job as an English teacher, extending my summer camp escapade into a full year! In line at the airport in Seoul, heading back to Tokyo, I had befriended a couple on a jet setter trip and invited them to my humble abode to get a taste of rural Japan. Unfortunately, the next morning I woke up running endlessly to the toilet and ended up spoiling the hospitality breakfast and a tour of the village I had planned for them. The husband was a doctor and left me his diarrhea remedy, warning me it was potent, but would calm my gut-wrenching pain. The couple left my apartment with a hand drawn map I made for them to continue their adventure and I was left with his little blue bottle of liquid; little did I know I would end up like Alice in Wonderland.

Alone on the weekend, no phone, and only a mini atlas to amuse myself, I began to daydream about a trip around the world. My mind slipped in and out of a delirious state, me on the edge of my futon, gripping my atlas, in this opium den ambience. Slowly I recovered from the first of many belly aches in Asia, but my crazy dream to traverse the globe started to slowly simmer in my heart. I lived a year in rural Japan until I felt I was ready to branch out. The dream of traveling around the world was still percolating deep inside. I needed more money, so I went to the cosmopolitan capital, Tokyo. What a crazy experience that turned out to be! (Hint: when a sumo wrestler grabs your arm and asks to dance in a Roppongi night club, don't refuse---the grip is REAL).

Tokyo was an all-night city, and I was initiated into the midnight pub crawl by another tourist (longtime resident). I had rented a room at "Michiko's" (a traditional old house converted into a youth hostel run by a daring Japanese woman) in the center of Tokyo; a backpacker's haven at the end of the line. Travelers from all over Southeast Asia had arrived tired, broke and hungry after a long jaunt around Asia. I was going the opposite direction, so I gathered stories and tips in case I wanted to head west to Europe. Japan was an amazingly safe country, but I wasn't sure about the rest of Asia. Stories of all sorts were startling and thrilling at the same time. I wasn't brave enough to go out on my own, given the tales I had heard. Most backpackers were flying directly home from Japan, so I had to find a companion on my own to start. I opted to ask Jill back in L.A., but she couldn't break away from her job just after getting her MBA. Nevertheless, she offered me her mother, Joan. Jill assured me that her mother would be a perfect match to begin my world traveling, given my youth and her experience. Joan had traveled in the Middle East and was eager to roam around Asia. Her husband preferred to stay at home in the comfort of the TV zone. My own mother was adventurous (not available for various reasons) so I understood how it might work.

Joan and I began to correspond by letters, and she turned out to be my cheerleader to take the plunge into a world backpacking trip. We agreed on China and Nepal. I set a date for a rendezvous in Hong Kong where we would tackle China together. No tours, no organized guides, just us as individual travelers. I borrowed my friend's mother and Joan borrowed her daughter's friend. Joan was willing to take a backpacker 30 years younger (me!) to fulfil her lifelong desire to see

China. I was glad to be traveling with a companion into 'communist China'. We were excited because China had just opened to individual travelers 2 years earlier, meaning we could go wherever we wanted without a guide (so I thought). You won't catch me on an organized tour; how boring!

In 1984 Mainland China was the hottest destination for backpacking trail blazers on the Southeast Asian route. China was the unknown territory that had been closed off to open tourism since 1949 (Mao's victory). Only in 1961 did diplomatic tours begin in China. Eventually, fully organized tours (non-diplomatic) were allowed in 1978. By 1982 independent travelers could venture on their own to certain destinations with mandatory permits stamped in their passports. So, when the book "China off the Beaten Track; How to do it on your own " made its debut, backpackers scrambled to get their hands on it; the only guidebook available for their unique style of roving around China (freelance).

We were going to be going way *off* the beaten track...

Prologue

I lie awake, hours ticking away before dawn breaks the twilight zone. It's insomnia, resulting from the sensation that there must be something I've forgotten to pack, an essential item, but what is it? Joan had packed balloons, pencils and erasers for the kids to help ease our lack of Chinese and make a good impression for diplomatic reasons. She had another perspective from her traveling experiences. I packed essentials, including my Swiss army knife and my yellow bandana, a piece of home that never gets left behind. There has to be something I've forgotten! It's just nerves, like my first trip to Asia heading to Hong Kong alone – that was definitely worse!

Actually, I was delighted to begin my dreamy world trip with a trusted companion (at least for the first part of my globe-trotting), even though we were the oddest couple on the road (24-year-old single woman and 54-year-old mother). Most of the backpackers were 20 something guys + 1 buddy, couples in their twenties, or lone male wolves. It never occurred to me that I was a woman, attempting to do it alone, an Amelia Earhart sort. Hopefully I won't be lost in the Bermuda triangle (or maybe Ms. Earhart just liked life better on an island away from great expectations).

Anyway tonight, here snuggled beneath the stars (my imagination), on a bunk bed under Joan (in a claustrophobic Hong Kong stale room), I was about to embark on the first leg of my world trip; a train to Canton, China. My life would never be the same, except maybe the stars, real or imaginary.

1

September 8, 1984

"Change your money". A whisper lands within my earshot as a man's shoulder brushes against mine like a Ninja swiftly identifying a mark. He pauses and swings back, maneuvering himself to drop into my other earlobe. Nothing new on the backpacker trail. I know this dance. Street money changers weave their way through crowds as they utter the secret code, "change your money". Meanwhile, banks sit on street corners like guards at the palace, silently at attention. Alternative money changers, there to beat the bank rates, set up shop down the road like vultures in a holding pattern. Giant scribbles on a board in plain view like score cards at a football game let the tourist know the latest price. But the freelance changer, wanting to break into the scene, daringly sweeps along the train station, cunningly avoiding the police; risky but cost effective; no paper, no electricity, no desk, nada de nada. Needless to say, they only need a close contact murmur to bait the target: "change". Best price wins, especially with cheap backpackers like me right now (easy with backpack on the floor, screaming 'here I am'). There isn't a bank or official money changer counter in sight. Oops, why didn't we change more money in Hong Kong? I had told Joan, my traveling companion, "We'll get a better rate once we're in China".

Arriving by train is romantic, but it does have a drawback; you are dumped at the end of the line to fend for yourself. The pages of this borrowed guidebook are marked with Emilio's handwriting. I'll never forget meeting Emilio in that extremely dubious hostel in Hong

Kong where we were all squeezed into a tiny dorm room (hole in the wall) with a unique bathroom set up. The shower hose was hooked up above the toilet, so you had to close the lid and sit or squat on the toilet to actually scrub-a-dub-dub. Emilio's bunk bed was above mine and he signaled I go ahead of him (backpacker chivalry), while the rest of the room was sleeping. Before that, I had never met an Italian here in Asia. When he suggested a western breakfast at MacDonald's after our freshening up, I was a bit reluctant. I had to admit, it was one of the few cheap choices we had available to us, and it would be a break from Chinese breakfast pork buns. When we sat down, he confessed he was partial to organic food. He was trained as a chemist but did not want to work on food additives, so he chose to focus on nutrition in hospitals and schools. I was astounded as I bit into my egg muffin, staring at the fast-food tray. He probably knew about all the crappy additives and their effects. But compromises when you are on the road are inevitable, and he knew it. He asked me if I knew about Rudolf Steiner, a well-known figure in European organic circles. I shook my head in ignorance and perked up listening to the fascinating biography of Steiner, and that is how our friendship began. I told him my plan to visit China, so he gave me a few tips. Emilio had been a guide for small groups when China had opened to individual travelers two years earlier. He offered his guidebook because he was leaving and didn't need it anymore. He was tired of touring Italians around China. Emilio said he would jot down some notes to help us, updating things from his recent trip (2 weeks ago). Thank goodness the book was in English and I could read his handwriting. I am now the caretaker of his beat-up copy of the bible for us daredevil travelers, called "China - Off the Beaten Track". Even Lonely Planet didn't have a section for China back in 1984 in its popular backpacker survival (must-have) guide, "Southeast Asia on a Shoestring". I made sure I had packed that book back in Hong Kong for the rest of my trip in Asia.

"Change your money, cheap!" According to the advice from 'Off the Track', cash was good to carry to start out in China. Given the fact that I was a sure target in a crowd of blue mao suits, the book claimed, "the money changers will find you." Let's get one thing straight, after 2 years in Japan, I knew I could not be mistaken or misread for 'Asian'. Misunderstood, yes! That's the double edge sword of traveling into the unknown, out of context, western garb or not---I was not Chinese. Foreign travelers are classified in two groups: Overseas Chinese (revisiting their motherland) and 'Others'. I wouldn't say I couldn't fit in even if I tried. It's not a question of language. Bluntly speaking, 5,000 years of culture accounts for a way of being. Asia is influenced by China or India (sometimes both). It's just a different world in the East.

Once you live in Asia, you realize there are more ways to do things. Writing without Roman letters, reading backwards from right to left, eating with wooden sticks and following the TAO, Confucius or the MAO, for example. Here in mainland China, 'other' means whoever isn't Chinese. Point blank; we are the 'others' and we can't fake it. First, round eyes are a dead giveaway even if you wear sunglasses to hide them. Comic books in Japan had been adopting this style of exaggerated round eyes for manga main characters as a cross-mix for modern life, especially the girls. Another clue is wearing 'western clothes' in China. Albeit most of the world was wearing similar attire (at least it wasn't a jogging suit!). I suddenly realize that in a 360-degree radius, all I can see is BLUE!

Joan is prepared with pencils, erasers and small trinkets for the kids. We can't speak, but we can smile as we hand out these small tokens as a gesture of friendship. That is the plan, anyway. "Change your money", the man cries as he circles back, and his breath lingers on my earlobe like a bad date from high school. I give up, no time to be fussy. We have a train to catch to Shanghai before dark. We need to change money and he knows it. I signal to him, and he is on my shoulder like a tai chi master lunging in for the final blow. Must be desperate. After all, I haven't seen a westerner anywhere on the train or here in the station. No one really notices us except the dubious money changer.

I am definitely not in Hong Kong anymore, where East and West collide in a convoluted harmony of Irish bars for happy hour and Chinese dim sum for breakfast. I am in Canton which could be described as a city with its hustle and bustle on par with Hong Kong. Although I have to admit it is actually "The People's Republic of China", as referred to in their terms. True, it is Chinese dominant, culturally speaking, but socially a whole different story. To us backpackers, it is 'Mainland China', since Taiwan and Hong Kong are independent territories on the fringe of the Chinese dragon tail (do not answer to Mainland China authority in 1984).

Joan had brought a 1979 National Geographic report of China (30 torn pages) along with a handy map provided as an insert. I am ready for an exploration into the back story of that glossy National Geographic photograph. Taiwan and Hong Kong just whet your appetite for Mainland China. Taiwan houses the national treasures (impressive and not to be missed) smuggled out by Chiang Kai-shek. The expert skills of Chinese artisans are absolutely unforgettable as one views the museum artistic treasures that attest to the renown Chinese cultural legacy. It was his last-ditch effort to save Chinese ancient art history from Mao's uprising of farmers that were easily swayed, considering the alternative: starving to death! Basic differences: Mao wanted to eradicate opium across the board.

Taiwan houses the national treasures (impressive and not to be missed) smuggled out by Chiang Kai-shek on his last-ditch effort to save the country from Mao's uprising of farmers that were easily swayed, considering the alternative: starving to death! Basic differences: Mao wanted to eradicate opium across the board. Chiang Kai-shek wasn't opposed to opium use for the aristocrats or upper classes (probably easier to manipulate and better than feudal wars). Mao realized that farmers would still be involved in the growing of poppy flowers if any law was lenient. The expert skills of Chinese artisans are absolutely unforgettable as one views the museum treasures in Taiwan and can attest to the Chinese cultural legacy. But those so-called 'treasures' pale in comparison to a good home cooked meal, or any semblance of civilized food beyond critters and morsels of rice.

Longstanding opium wars, import taxes, and international power jockeying devastated the Chinese countryside by turning away from imports towards domestic cultivation of opium, enticing farmers with market demands. Replacing food crops (rice, soybeans, etc.) with opium had a short-term effect: high profits (gold standard) and starvation! Let's face it, Chinese cuisine has been cultivated for millennia with special herbs, spices, and techniques aimed at a 'long life'. Naturally, the average age for 'longevity' would increase with proper food supplies, except for infectious diseases or plagues. Starving by design with basic crops replaced with highly valued poppy flowers (opium) can set up an unbearable likeness of a roadblock to 'longevity'. Canton, as a southern port city, was a controversial gateway for smugglers competing for a foothold in the prized poppy flower market (I am not talking about a floating flower market). We are standing in the middle of an historical hub of the opium wars, and we are totally oblivious.

I leave Joan behind at the train station, so I can follow the money changer, to where? We divide the tasks. She is to buy our first train tickets to embark on our Chinese exploration. Joan is a seasoned traveler disguised as an innocent homemaker on holiday, when in fact she is like a secret antique dealer on the prowl. She is used to wheeling and dealing for a bargain. She took me on as her apprentice, so I could learn the ropes of how to pick through the junk and unearth a worthy relic that would be considered 'valuable' back home. {I still have a giant wooden rice spoon negotiated from a rural Chinese woman's kitchen; it was plucked right out of the rice cooker, hot and sticky! Joan didn't care, no need to wash it, just bargain and keep moving}.

My money changer man is into power walking, leading me to some unknown destination. He's moving faster than a pheasant dodging a hunter's pursuit as he swiftly turns corners, checking his back to make sure his big 'fish' is still on the hook. I am smiling, the only way to communicate. I do not know any Chinese. What an idiot! I didn't study a lick of Chinese before the trip, only a bit of historical data. China had been closed to tourism (outside of diplomatic visits) from 1949 until 1978. China, a strangely controlled country that had supposedly emancipated its people from growing opium for foreign trade (don't forget all those vintage photos of opium dens and wild imaginations of writers) by going back to growing rice for the common folk. Joan had talked about stories she had heard about bodies floating down the Yangtze River before the Mao revolution. I haven't noticed any starving people, yet.

I follow the scent of the money changer's whisper in and out of alleys, faster and faster. What's his hurry? I woke up at the crack of dawn in Hong Kong to catch the train to Canton. "Hey, wait up." I'm carrying my passport around my neck under my blouse, as a precaution, with my dollars and official travelers' checks. Joan is back at the station with our bags. My money changer stops inside a patio of an apartment building no more than 3 stories high. "Wait here." I wonder where he is going. Probably he's going to his house to get the stash to make the exchange; it's a chance we both have to take (typical black-market tactics; lead you to their territory out of sight of authorities). Minutes feel like hours, and I am starting to doubt this idea.

Where am I? I can't even begin to remember the way back to the train station. A woman screams from the 2nd floor balcony, ">>>>>" in Chinese, pointing at me. The money changer comes down with a gunny sack big enough to store rice for a full winter. He opens it quickly. It's full of crumpled cash! Shit! You expect me to walk out of here nonchalantly with this sack? I look at him dumbfounded (I was really dumb!). Not to mention that it is 'people's' money, not the official tourist currency. I say, "What's this?" He blurts out, "Change! Hurry!" People are coming out of their apartments looking down at me, the woman still screaming "<<<<" and everyone is pointing at me! I panic and run out. I do not want to be picked up by authorities on my first landing in the country. Luckily, I am wearing jogging shoes for this trip!

"Train station?" "Train station?" I am dodging carts and bicycles packed to the gills, women with children everywhere, pushcarts with loads of rice in sacks like the one I just left behind. Now I am having second thoughts. I can fit it in quite nicely on a cart, if I don't panic. But then how will I travel around China with this rice bag full of unofficial money? And a backpack? No, it is good I left the money changer in the dust, waving his hands. I am sweating and running on nerves! Nothing in the book about this situation. I am way, way, way off the beaten track. All I can catch sight of is a sea of blue mao suits. I stop anyone who will listen to me, to ask for directions. "Train station?" People point me in the direction of the couples, women, young students. Finally, I stop asking and just follow the trail of Chinese travelers, as I figure out that they are heading for the train station, too! In fact, it seems like lots of people are heading out of town.

I'm stumbling in the late summer/early autumn heat, on the verge of a nervous breakdown. How could I be so stupid to get so far away from the train station alone! This is China, not Hong Kong! Panting like a puppy dog off the leash on its first run around the block, coming home with its tail between its legs, I look for Joan. Joan is easy to spot (she's a tall, blond woman with round eyes and not wearing BLUE). There she is! Joan's still standing guard with our bags. I pant, "Joan, did you get the tickets? Let's go!" I had lost everyone on my sprint back to the station and I wanted to kiss my tennis shoes. Let's face it, Birkenstocks wouldn't have cut the grade on this jaunt! Joan sheepishly replies, "No, I couldn't get up to the counter". We are standing there in the middle of a crowded Chinese train station, without a clue. "OK, don't worry, I've got my Chinese dictionary." I wiggle myself to the counter through a massive Chinese cacophony. China has a one child plan for a reason! Overpopulation! Finally, I get to the counter with a billion people bearing down on my neck: sweating (all of us together), pushing me over the counter, yelling to the clerk over my head. I fumble through my dictionary. After defending my position (using my basketball skills) for what seems like eternity, two tickets fly through the porthole. GOAL!

2

All aboard! Joan and I are piled into the train like two flies caught up in a beehive by accident. The worker bees are swirling around, apparently in a free-for-all effort to get a seat. We have our seats assigned and printed on the tickets, so a train station attendant takes us to them when he notices we are almost being trampled at the door; then he suddenly escapes! I am confused. I observe the other passengers frantically shifting bags on the overhead rack, grabbing packages and cloth wrapped bundles; even babies are passed over my head through the window! What the heck? After the commotion, it seems that all that pushing and pulling has nothing to do with first come, first sit policy. They actually *DO* have seat assignments! I guess the rush was for the overhead rack space (a rare commodity). Luckily our bags have been hoisted up rapidly by the train attendant, like a speedy pole vault champion.

I have little to nil experience of long train journeys, other than the Tokyo high speed bullet train to Kyoto. I could barely finish my lunch as the countryside whipped by on the famous Tokaido trail that Japanese rave about as a 'poetic trail'. I was often reminded of Basho, the traditional haiku poet/retired general/monk who had meandered his way along the 500 kilometers on foot, inspired by its beauty to create original poetry. He had time to pause and contemplate a water-fall dribbling over moss covered rocks; awakening his consciousness. My bullet train experience was one of diminishing returns, neither poetic nor inspiring. No time to mingle, get a cup of tea, or enjoy the scenery. It was just a blur in the latest Japanese high-tech experience. We Americans are getting over the stigma of 'Made in Japan' with price wars gaining momentum and leading people to accept imported electronics because they are massively affordable. Back in the 70's, I remember my dad coming home with a cassette player; not just one for the family but three! One for each of us kids. We had never had such personal gifts popping up out of the blue. Those were made in Japan and must have been a good deal. I mean Dad came waltzing into the house, unannounced, with bundles to open on a sunny afternoon in Spring. My parents are never extravagant nor whimsical. I remember wondering if mine was going to break after a week. Nope, I had it up until university (years of fast forward, rewind, and eject). I even knew how to manually rewind my jumbled cassettes with a pencil, a skill I picked up in high school. I finally outgrew it, but to my surprise it did not break. This is the vast difference so far as I can notice between China and Japan. China appears to be frozen in time, while Japan is manufacturing from A-Z faster than anyone can blink.

Joan manages to squeeze into our window seat and, soon we are knobbing knees with the locals. We are pleased with the seats we bought on our first train trip. By the way, it is a 3rd class 'hard-seat'. Joan had wanted these seats so we would be in the midst of the 'locals' so as to soak up the experience to the fullest. She thrives on the un-adulterated cultural experiences, even if it means a risky situation, like when she stayed to the end of the evacuation of westerners during the Iran revolution in the late 70's! Back to our train seats, I would have to describe the hard-seat train ticket in China as 'raw' and down to earth; survival of the fittest. I watch as young mothers squat in the door-ways with their bundled-up infant (one child) on their knees. At first, I think, how absurd! Why don't they have priority for a seat? And I would soon find out why! Next to the mothers on the other end of the doorway passage was a humongous hot water boiler with a spout. That seemed incredibly dangerous!

During this maiden voyage, after the first hour I noticed people getting up to get a cup of hot water from the boiler. Good idea! We had packed our own mugs and cutlery for hygienic reasons. Now they come in handy. We fit right in, except our mugs are not government issued, enamel glazed over tin? (I'm guessing). Ours are plastic (handy to wash and dry) baby mugs, with cartoon motifs. Actually hokey, plastic (kid) cups! Anyway, I get up to get my free lunch (hot water!). As I am filling up our mugs, Joan is quietly enjoying the landscape in a trance by the window. Suddenly, my shoes are getting soaked in baby piss, as a mother gently holds up her baby with an open crotch to piss next to me. There are no diapers (disposable or cotton nappies) in China? Are these mothers in China clairvoyant when it comes to 'potty training'? She smiles and I smile back, considering this is our only mutual set of language skills. Ingenious plan! A diaper-free country! No landfills full of diapers, no diaper service, less work for the mothers or fathers. Diaper changing wiped away! Nobody seems to mind the yellow river, so I go with the FLOW! My first Tao lesson (#1).

Our train companions are so up close and personal, sitting on the old-fashioned, wooden bench and laughing, staring at us and enjoying the novelty of foreign women. Mind you, Joan and I look like mother and daughter to them (age wise). Anybody from our home country would never think that I (Latina) and Joan (English-Scottish-Norwegian mix) were even slightly related. I notice the guy in front of me is wearing a neon, hot pink tank top under his green mao suit. It catches my interest in this country of 'sameness', at least on the exterior. In this overwhelming sea of uniformity, you can't help but focus on the faces and eyes of people rather than their superficial clothing style.

I was already a supporter of used clothes; less is more in the overconsumption of seasonal wardrobes and energy waste from manufacturing textiles, an idea I gradually embraced. First it was by necessity from vintage hunting at thrift shops, and secondly from working during college in a factory, weaving cloth for medical cast material. Once I saw the enormous mechanical weaving machines set to 24 hours non-stop, I was aware of how much energy consumption was involved in textile production.

But here in BLUE China, this concept is taken to a whole new level of simplification. Less time to get dressed in the morning before work, *'freedom from choice'*, like the Devo punk song. The tiny fragment of neon color beneath this blue façade struck me as a slight individual choice. The concept of a division between 'white collar' and 'blue collar' (workers) is obliterated from the start. What I see so far is that everyone here is a blue-collar worker; level down across the board. Later I would find out the differences between the blue and green mao suits. The rare grey colored mao suits are hidden from public view, given that they are reserved for government officials behind the scenes.

How did I know about the grey suits? Later I'll explain how we were stopped on a train detour by accident and pulled into a police station on the way to Dali; a small village in the backcountry. It was an innocent mix up, but the consequence was crazy! That situation occurred later, on our way back from the western territories. Here on this train, it is roughly 80% blue and 20% green. We were told the green was military garb, but anyone could get one (so fake military?). Kinda like the fashion statement back home of camouflage that people picked up at the used military outlets. That fashion started in the 1970's with the fallen soldiers in Vietnam, and then market demand; sturdier and cheaper than Levi blue jeans. Army boots became more popular with time and morphed into the Dr. Martens version. Here, I am not sure if clothes are government assigned in the classic blue Mao rations, and the extra outfits can be bought. It's always confusing learning the codes of a new country.

According to my calculations we are due to arrive in Shanghai in about 8 hours. So, we settle in with our new 'friends' and play a lot of charades. How else are we going to communicate? Joan is trying to explain about our trip but with no luck. I am trying to convey some other ridiculous idea. In the end we are all laughing from the miscommunication. The wheels keep turning, clicky click, and who knows if we will ever get to Shanghai. I am re-filling our mugs with hot water. Joan tries to play a game where we clap hands with each other and with our guests on the other side of the bench. It is a game of no words and only coordination with a bit of intuition. It helps break the ice and passes the time. Joan muses, "Did you get that?" "I dunno know what he's saying?" We shrug and laugh it off to keep the semblance of dialogue going smoothly.

After about 3 hours, hunger starts to set in. While our companions take out their lunch boxes and chopsticks, we head to the dining car. That is the one luxury we allow ourselves on this trip. Hard seat to travel, but dining car to eat. As the train swerves from rail to rail like a snake in the grass, we navigate our way down the carriages. Finally, we arrive at the dining car where we stop to catch our breath. Can you imagine what it is like stumbling through an overcrowded Chinese train? (An obstacle course that's moving at 60 miles per hour!).

On a train with about a billion and one travelers, 3 tables are taken. We hadn't made reservations, but the 12 empty tables are at our disposal. We sit down to a freshly starched linen tablecloth and elegant silverware, with a fragrant candle as the centerpiece. The table is poetically lit with low romantic lighting, gorgeous wooden panels on the walls, and velvet cushioned seats. I feel as if we have gone back to the 1920's rolling along on Agatha Christie's *Orient Express* train. On the way to the toilet in the back of the dining car, I pass the kitchen. It is amazing to see a full staff cooking fresh meals on this wavering train heading into the sunset. We order from the limited menu, which includes plum wine. It is our first dabble in Chinese cuisine outside Hong Kong.

Our first dishes arrive; a whiff of scrumptious aromas rises into my face like a fragrant steam bath. I take no time to mix the garlic, tangy cayenne, spicy eggplant with my hardy, Chinese rice, cooked to perfection (not too soggy, not too sticky). It hits my tongue with delight and I am astounded at the delicacy that tingles my palate. Already I'm thinking Chinatown restaurants set up by Chinese exiles and refugees back home, never could compare to this dining experience. I feel like I have never really experienced Chinese cooking before this meal! Joan explains to me the unique traditional farming method that she knows from her father's stories that gives me a sweet and sour taste in my mouth as I am starting my second course. "They use 'honey pots' for fertilizer, so it's totally organic", she explains. I am thrilled to learn about fresh farm veggies with no commercial fertilizers. Innocently, I ask, "What are honey pots?" Joan quickly explains to me what they are. She continues, "Have you ever seen farmers carrying two buckets with a wooden yoke on their shoulders through the fields?" I keep eating the delicious bright green bok choy, nodding in agreement. She smirks. "Well, those are full of human feces, fermented of course." I almost choke on my 'organic' greens! "What are you saying?" She is smiling. "I heard they used to call them honey pots because it was better than referring to it literally, don't you think?" My jaw is already dropping, and I am looking for an open window to vomit. "Are you kidding?" Joan tries to comfort me, "Don't worry, it's perfectly safe. It's a tradition carried down for generations." I lose my appetite, and take a giant gulp of the plum wine, thinking the fruit is too far away on a tall tree to be hit with splattered 'honey'. After feeling tipsy, I move on to dessert. It looks edible and vegetable free. I check the menu, soy cake...I'll pass. Joan giggles as I pass up dessert and orders her soy cake. I would get used to the 'organic' methods of China, sooner or later. After all, do I have a choice?

I then begin to realize that back home all those 'wastewater' treatment centers are basically based on the same concept. The crossover to urban planning is now part of the 'progressive' ecological drought solution in southern California. I remember a project in a new residential development area that was a research extension of my university. It went like this... "lavender spigots" as a coded method (kinda cute color) were installed as the icon to caution residents not to drink the water. Soon after, wastewater was recycled for watering lawns. Now that's a waste! A veggie garden is a much more sustainable use of the land. I had studied social ecology, and nobody was interested in my degree in 1982, so I am traveling to see the world. Nonetheless, on this train slicing through the rice fields, I am completing a circle; seeing the origins of 'social ecology' up close and personal (my plate is still barely touched), dating back surely thousands of years. Weird loophole in the universe. Tao lesson #2: What goes around, comes around.

We drink more wine, watching the beginning of sunset over the Chinese countryside, with shadows of farmers carrying their swishing honey pots. How romantic, you say. I am just traumatized, and it is only the beginning of the 'authentic Chinese cuisine' experience. We weave ourselves back to our hard seat and everyone is starting to pack to leave the train. Are we already in Shanghai? How exciting! Pulling into the station, I think, what a small track. I could only see two platforms. This is weird. I ask our companions as the train slows down, "Shanghai?" They shake their heads, and say, "Hangzhou". I turn to Joan. "Where are we?" She pulls out her giant National Geographic map, which is bigger than the window. Suddenly people are shuffling and pushing each other as the train passengers head for the doors, the nearest exodus. I tell her to just put it away, that we can straighten everything out once we are in the station. After stares from all corners of the train she folds it up and stuffs it into her hand bag. I am sure we will find help to get on our way to Shanghai. Luckily, Joan has brought a map! We are good with a map and dictionary, plus our handy "Off the Beaten Track" bible. What can go wrong?

3

It is obvious we have not pulled into Shanghai, considering the utter smallness of the station and less than 3 million people milling around. We are confused. Maybe we have to change trains? I go to the counter to inquire about the next train. Meanwhile, Joan stands by our bags. When I turn around to check on her, I see she is surrounded by a crowd, and handing out pencils to the kids! They are all touching her gently like she's an animal at a petting zoo, and she is smiling. I stride up to the counter. I have my dictionary ready, and tickets in hand. I look at the map above the counter and it seems to me that we are close to Shanghai, so I am confident there is only some kind of a small glitch here.

Nothing is what it appears to be in foreign countries, and it is here in Hangzhou that I learn my first word in Chinese (repeated over and over). Considering the intonation in southern China is crucial with 9 tones; repetition is key to getting the right flavor of the word (common mistake: 'Ma' said one way is HORSE, another way is MOTHER!). Actually, the dialect gives me a headache most of the time, with its extreme highs and lows swinging, ringing, piercing your eardrums like acrobats whizzing overhead! Mandarin, however, is sweeter to my ears. How could I not remember "Meiyo"? It is quite versatile: "No, we don't have it, No, we don't do it, No, it's impossible, No I can't, No you can't, No we can't." Latin conjugation, it seems to me, is overly complicated. This language is simple for all people, places and things. No is NO! Meiyo!

Next train to Shanghai? "Meiyo". I point at the words in my dictionary as I point at the tracks. "Which track, please?" The dreaded "Meiyo." My puzzled face and ridiculous Chinese get me directed to a side office. Looking back at Joan, I see she is fine with entertaining the group with gestures while holding down the fort with our bags. Quickly I scoot over to the CITS (printed on the door) to try and get some answers. It is the famous Chinese International Tourist Service, originally set up for diplomats and organized tours. Basic instructions in English could be helpful in an emergency, says my book. It pointed out that not all cities have this service. For some reason, Hangzhou seems important enough to have an office, thank goodness!

Stepping inside with a bit of caution, I inquire by showing my tickets to an 'official'. China is not Japan and people are rather straightforward. I was hit in the face with this reality when stepping off the boat from Japan and arriving in Taiwan. It was a 'rude' awakening of people pushing, yelling, and no one paying attention to manners (Japan is overly polite). Hey, but in these crucial moments, better to forgo the formalities and get right down to it. The official attendant bluntly responds, "Your tickets stop here." I eagerly replied, "no problem, we can buy more tickets." "Meiyo", chimes in an assistant. "Excuse me?" "There are no tickets." So now I am getting worried: "No tickets to Shanghai?" Short and curt: "Sold out." "Really?" "Meiyo", chimes in the little guy (again). Basic translation spews out: "It's the Moon Festival. Everyone going home." I repeat, "Moon Festival?". "Yes, big family festival." I push on: "When can we go to Shanghai? Any tickets?" Tactical answer: "In 2 days." I am astonished! Restating the obvious, "2 days! We want to go tonight!" Now a chorus of clerks are chanting, "Meiyo". Actually, I do not understand 'Meiyo', yet, but I am starting to get the hang of it. "Do you want a ticket for day after tomorrow?" I figure it's the best we can do. I surrender. "Yes, please." I push the CITS (China International Travel Service) glass doors open, tickets in hand. Defeated.

Back to the three-ring circus around Joan. I wiggle my way to her side and break the bad news to her, "We are stuck here for two days." Everyone in the crowd is happy to see me, reaching out, lightly touching my arms and hair. Welcome to China 1984! We sure are a novelty in this town! I start flipping through 'Off the Beaten Track' to find out where to stay. I report to Joan, "It says there is only 1 tourist hotel for 'others' and 1 hotel for Overseas Chinese". Bingo… freedom from choice. Joan starts gesturing for a hotel and I point in my dictionary to a woman in the pack. This should be easy, can't get lost with this swarm escorting us to the 'only tourist hotel in town'. Gleefully, we are parading through the streets. Pretty fast, we find ourselves in front of the official tourist hotel. Joan waves goodbye to the crowd of people who have followed us and I loosen myself from the many naïve curious hands clinging to me (mostly women and children). Quickly I read the guidebook to get an idea of what's available in terms of rooms and best options. "Dorm rooms are cheap, if the hotel has one. Next best option is a double room to share costs." I shut the book and I am ready to approach the counter to get settled into our room. I am dead tired from heaps of novel experiences and an overload of Chinese shouting, so I'm just looking forward to rest up a couple of days before our trip to Shanghai. I circle the words in the dictionary to move on quickly in order to secure two beds in a dorm or a double room, just in case. Easier said than done. Little do I know; non-verbal communication will be sufficient with no need for any type of translation. Joan has the advantage; she is deaf in one ear. So, I suffer in stereo from the endless echo of a repeated refrain from the hotel reception staff: "Meiyo."

How is it possible there are no rooms available? No beds? This is the only tourist joint in town for westerners and I hadn't seen anybody on the streets that even resembled us. No matter how many times I explain our dilemma and state the obvious that there is 'no other' hotel, the chorus of 'Meiyo' is sternly grunted. There are about 12 hotel staff personnel standing around in the lobby doing absolutely nothing but watching this frustrating scene. I signal Joan to sit down on the nice chairs in front of us. I whisper, "Joan, we have to wait it out." I read in the book that you have to insist on rooms, because no one wants to do any extra work. Of course, our stay would imply preparing the room, tidying up, and eventually cleaning the room. It is crystal clear we are not in a customer service venue with any commercial aspects. The staff is paid whether they work or not. Simple Simon. I can play their game. I whisper to Joan, "It takes two to tango!"

The dance begins, as we sit for 30 minutes, and then I stand up and go to the receptionist to inquire again. "Meiyo". No matter what I ask, the response is a broken record in unison. They can keep a straight face, too! I am quite impressed. We sit down again. 30 minutes later, I go again to the counter. "Any rooms come available?" This time I do not even try to use Chinese. "Meiyo". Joan repeats 'meiyo' to me. I am ready to jump the counter. Joan snickers. She has a good spirit about cross-cultural misunderstandings. Our guidebook says, just keep your cool and insist politely, because they have to serve you. I follow suit with all the patience I can rally together, considering the day is dragging on like a Rocky moment in the boxing ring. We are all running circles around the 'meiyo' bush, and finally our tango subsides after only 3 hours. The book said sometimes it can take up to half a day, so I feel like a winner! Finally, it is obvious we are not leaving until we have beds, so the defeated receptionist, ignoring my eyes, points to her left. "Follow that woman". Joan lifts her head from the guidebook and says, "She meido" - thank you." Only one of the 12 staff nods. The rest look disappointed by the outcome, probably thinking 'more work for us!' I see Joan had been studying during the showdown. I am impressed. Why hadn't I thought of that instead of wasting my time on dirty looks? From this point on, I am inspired to learn Chinese. Indeed, I am good at languages if I put my mind to it. So, the Chinese language immersion course begins. I perk up my ears and take pride in the fact that I have already learned "Meiyo" and "she-she". I'm just scared of the operetta range of tones in Cantonese and possible lost ideas in translation. Soon we will be leaving southern China and Mandarin will be music to my ears!

The woman who escorts us to the room is silent and efficient. That seems like the most we can expect in this hotel. We have to carry our own bags, and considering the fiasco we encountered at the front desk neither one of us is in the mood for tipping. They would never guess what they missed, as we are big tippers! Too bad, they'll never know! So, we just smile as she opens the door and hands Joan the key. No sooner do we enter and the woman leaves our room, I collapse on the bed. It seems like ages since we have been in a reclining position, and it feels wonderful!

Joan has been reading about the town while I was negotiating our room. Joan announces to me that the famous 'West Lake' district has its own unique cuisine, suggesting we go out for a bite to eat. But it is getting late and I can't make a move. I shake my head and utter, "okay, tomorrow". At least we have a bed! There's no chance we will starve tonight, considering we have our handy oatmeal packets for emergencies. I plug in my hot water gadget that heats up water one cup at a time (a must on the backpacker trail!) Then, Joan notices a teapot and hot water maker on the table. Of course, we are in China, it's a staple food/drink here. Well, it is flavored or regular oatmeal for our bedtime snack. Joan takes the unflavored and I opt for cinnamon; my standard comfort spice when homesick. Slurping up our porridge, we check the maps in 'Off the Beaten Track' and can see the lake is relatively nearby. We discuss taking a stroll to the lake for lunch tomorrow. We have two days to kill time, anyway. Tonight, I sleep like a bear in hibernation, reluctant to begin the next day in 'meiyo' land.

Today Joan is up bright and early, ready to discover Hangzhou. She is reading to me as I lie limp on the relatively brand new-firm mattress. I am content to wallow in my den. Excitedly, she explains the history of the place. "This city is a famous getaway for the people of Shanghai to meet". She continues, "Important political exchanges happened right here!" I, however, am worn thin from the previous day of historical cultural interchanges from the train station, the money changing debacle, and the battle at the hotel reception desk. I finally muster up enough energy to get up and head to the toilet. Strangely enough, my stomach and intestines are quite happy. I feel good from the food I ate the night before, so that is a plus. Diarrhea is prominent in Asia, to the point of near death. I guess the authentic 'honey pot-organic' Chinese food agreed with me! Now I can't deny that fact!

Ready or not we are headed to 'West Lake' for lunch. Joan reads that the famous 'west lake fish' is a delicacy not to be missed, and she's set on trying it. The book says, order one, as they are large and plenty for 2-3 people. Wow! I am getting intrigued with this aspect of meal-time. So, we take to the streets and head to the lake for our big fish! To our surprise, West Lake is an anomaly in the midst of blue-collar Mao China. We come upon a picturesque landscape with various pavilions connected by walkways of crimson red bridges. I am totally taken aback by this spectacular landscape before my eyes! It's like a 'Golden Gate' Kodak moment (Kodak and Fuji film are competing at this time). I prefer Fuji film for my camera because it captures the tropical colors better than Kodak.

I had bought a fairly expensive Canon AL1 with an added 35-75mm lens and sky filter. My friend in Japan, who is a professional photographer, picked it out for me before this China trip. Here I carry my camera nonchalantly in my shoulder bag with a towel while on the streets, so as not to draw attention to my modest lens and camera case. I believe in interacting with people and then photographing them as a cultural exchange rather than as a secret intrusive observer with a super telescopic lens. And slides are my preference rather than photos. They are versatile and can be turned into photos. Best option in 1984.

It turns out that Hangzhou was the first destination to be promoted by the Chinese government for tourism in 1961 (diplomats and overseas Chinese). It is delicately carved out of a storybook to impress foreigners like us. We sit down to a linen tablecloth and the waiters speak fluent English. With diplomatic manners they kindly help us decide on a meal. Joan enquires about 'West Lake fish' and all heads nod in agreement that it is a specialty of the area. I love fish, so it is fine by me. The waiters also suggest other dishes to accompany the fish. Our breakfast was scant, as we wanted to leave quickly to avoid the hotel reception staff. Now we are content and looking forward to our long-awaited lunch on the lake. Considering the substantial delay, we are beginning to think that maybe they are fishing; really fresh catch of the day! Meanwhile, we are listening to the waves lightly swooshing against the platform, enjoying a clear day of sunshine, and not worrying about a thing. Then, the grand moment arrives; a huge fish on a platter with a garnishing fit for the last emperor is placed before our eyes. I love chopsticks; when eating fish, they are always preferable to a fork. Politely, I signal Joan to take the first bite. I am starving, but age before beauty, as the saying goes. Joan puckers up and takes a sizable bite from the center of the fish, and I will never forget her face. She slowly turns her eyes to me and murmurs, "You gotta try it." She has a full mouth, so she can't say much. I get it. I just have to try it myself. I whittle my chopsticks into the belly of the decorated centerpiece of a fish right before my eyes. It smells fresh and steaming with ginger essence. Joan is fumbling for her napkin, wiping her mouth. I am shocked! I take a bite. It is fishy alright, but the greasy, fatty tissue of this poor old fish starts drooling from my mouth like a chunk of lard! Joan is spitting out the fish in her napkin, ever so diplomatically. I can only play along. Acting as if nothing is wrong, we ask for a takeout box to bring back to the hotel for 'dinner'. The restaurant staff smiles and are very obliging. Quickly I maneuver my chopsticks to nonchalantly heave slices of ginger into my mouth to clean my palate. Joan is shaking her head in agreement to follow my lead; nobody even has a clue about our unpleasurable reaction! We order plum wine to wash down the big fat fish. Finally, we take a taxi back to the hotel to forget about that greasy fish, and not to mention we are slightly tipsy.

I am stuffed to the gills, so to speak. Not actually from the lunch, but more from the nausea arising from the overfill of ginger and plum wine. Food is usually an integral part of the delights of visiting cultures beyond the confines of a living room TV food show, or the newspaper travel section. You see a chef preparing the complicated dishes and people wiping their lips ever so carefully with an afterglow on their face, only leaving traces of the food on their plate. The appealing rundown of scheduled shows tempts us to wanna be there, eat there, book my trip! I'd say it's the reason we travel over the seven seas, put up with knee cramps (I'm talking about economy 'class'), opt for flight patterns that could be considered illogical due to the 'price is right' and of course the odd hours we reluctantly bear including, but not limited to, layovers, stopovers, sleep deprivation; only to repeat to a new exciting locale. How did we get from the appealing food section of our TV guide to a lush fish plopped on a platter that should have been put on weight watchers' lean diet? Did we miss something? I am hoping Shanghai has a larger tasting menu. Maybe we should try to catch part of the Moon Festival delicacies. I'd go for some dessert later on. Skipping a meal from time to time may do us some good. Joan opens the taxi door and drags me out. She informs me she is going to take a 'siesta'; Mexican style short nap.

We have recovered from our 'big fish' lunch with our siesta. It's time for dinner, but I prefer to only look for dessert. I go downstairs to the lobby to check out what's going on for the Moon Festival. It's more of an excuse to stretch my legs, given I feel I had been on the bench in a baseball game for hours in the train. I meet a guy who says he's been here for a couple of days taking photos of the Moon Festival. He encourages me to experience this rare moment that coincides with this Chinese tradition and points me in the direction of a nearby street. He assures me that it is perfectly (basically) safe to take a stroll to observe for myself. After all, the Moon Festival is only once a year and the most important event in this season. It celebrates the rice harvest and is like Christmas with everyone returning to their hometowns to be with family and friends. Not to mention the illusion that the moon is close to earth and appears larger than usual.

I go back upstairs to relay the message to Joan, but she prefers to stay in the hotel and rest. I tell her I won't be long and it's not that late, anyway. I walk alone and listen to the stones under my feet that make a rattle. I don't take my camera because I want to be immersed in the festival. I can hear singing here and there like birds on a spring day. I am surrounded by a mist hovering over the green hills with crumbling clay houses. I feel so much better in the night air. I am not really focused on dessert, but rather just a casual stroll without a care in the world.

The festivities are part of the fabric of this ancient culture, which is a surprise given the Cultural Revolution. I suppose the actual cultural revolution that China experienced in the aftermath of Mao's victory honed in on the intellectual and religious leaders. It's part of the dogma that states 'religion is for the masses' as a control or distraction to the real problems (not like football games or baseball heroes lined up for the World Series---sports mania religion). Who would ever imagine that God would have to be lumped into a debate on labor issues. Couldn't better wages, decent conditions, and adequate housing regardless of spiritual inclinations be a consideration without dogma here and there?

Back on the unbeaten track, on this lonely planet meander, the oversized moon is drenching my evening with a pleasant detour from overthinking. Even though people are staring at me, I take my time on the last leg back to the hotel; I don't sense any danger. I notice some young Chinese guys on bicycles stopped outside a group of houses. They seem innocent. One is holding a guitar. I ask him to play by motioning with my hands. He answers, "No, no" and hands the guitar to me---humming a tune. Soon his friend comes forward on another bike and I give the guitar to him. This young guy takes the guitar reluctantly, but then begins to play and sing a beautiful Chinese melody---I won't forget his face with his dark hair and mustache. He is singing with such emotion even while his friends continue to talk. I wave goodbye and lazily amble back to the hotel; I have just been serenaded in Chinese. There is a first time for everything.

I lay in bed pondering our trip so far. In the middle of this 'communist' country, I am finding people are friendly, kind and openly sharing their heartfelt emotions with us. The BLUE overall picture fades quickly with smiles and helpful gestures along the way as we find the pieces of the jigsaw puzzle on this journey. Mind you, not everyone is on the same page of kindness, but as strangers in a new land we haven't encountered any sense of criminal meanness or violence that could potentially ruin our trip. We may not understand what the heck is going on (most of the time) because we just haven't had any 6 o'clock news reports from this side of the world for eons.

I pick up Snow's book to the pass the time with the energetic, full moon keeping me up. I am reading how he describes the 'communist revolution' as an overzealous plan and a "somewhat quixotic expedition...blocked by Generalissimo Chiang Kai-Shek...but had not prevented patriotic students courting imprisonment or possible death...uttering the forbidden slogans: "Cease civil war! Cooperate with the Communists to resist Japan! Save China!"...One midnight I climbed aboard a dilapidated train...I was bound for 'Red China'. And a little ill because I had taken all the inoculations available...alarming reports had lately told of the spread of bubonic plague...one of the few spots on earth where it was endemic." Snow and I were in an unknown territory; however, his travel diary is overly political, and referred to as 'The Classic Account of the Birth of Chinese Communism'. There is nothing poetic or even anthropological so far in his book. Me on the other hand am here as a curious bystander with hardly a clue. I heard the 'Iron Curtain' and 'Red China' labels blurting out from the newscaster at dinnertime back home. I was somewhere between the *Sounds of Silence* marking the end of the Vietnam war and the confusion of where's the real capital of China on the geopolitical map? In Taipei, Hong Kong, or Peking (Beijing)? I wouldn't say we were informed about Asia to any real/news reel extent.

Our family tribe did not regularly watch TV growing up apart from Felix the Cat, Gumby, Road Runner, and Soul Train (dance moves) on Saturday mornings. We were an anomaly in L.A. that revolved around Hollywood movies, TV stars and after-school shows. News was a different story. Background music for dinner was the soundtrack to the news; I had the seat with my back to the screen. When I could see, I liked to watch the weather reports because I loved clouds. It was a hobby I shared with my father to identify formations, such as cirrostratus, in the morning before school looking outside at the sky together. The biggest news event I remember that we watched as a family was the rocket launch of Apollo 11 to the moon. It was a time to sit around the TV, quiet and at full attention. I don't know if it was only because my father's company had some part in the thermally resistant materials used for the extremely high temperatures during take-off or an American big deal. Looking at the moon last night, it brought back memories of those emotional moments as a kid.

Here, on the other side of the globe, the simple tradition of moon gazing together is reenacted without all the high-tech TV cameras. Delicious mooncakes are made from ancient recipes and eaten to mark a festive time. The moon gleaming, smiling brightly to everyone alike (you almost wished you could turn down the light!). Even so far away up in the sky, it radiated unsurpassed beauty, creating an illusion. Only the naked eye could grasp the grand essence of its translucent glow and lock it away into our hearts (no awkward space boots); leaving no footprint per se. Nonetheless it leaves an inspiration for a brief Haiku poem with a Chinese melody echoing in my heart chamber. China has me frozen in time. I am dozing off to sleep in a moon shadow mood.

This morning, the sun is beating down on our window. I suppose the moon has already set on the horizon, while Joan is shaking me out of my dreamy state. "Wake up, lazy bones", she kids me. I am suddenly back to reality and back on the 'beaten track' to get on with our travel plan. Joan has picked out our itinerary; we are going for a walk to find a silk factory. On the way, we see children on their way to school; up until now we've only seen kids hanging out with their mothers. These students are wearing red short scarves around their necks and carrying books in their arms (no mothers in sight). There are two girls and two boys with their rubber boots and a big black umbrella singing a song. The girls stop to look at a big flower with velvety petals---a gorgeous magenta color that stands out in the midst of greys and browns of crumbling houses. They bend down to get a closer look at this enticing flower. I ask if I can take a picture and they nod 'yes'. It is a unique moment with their innocent faces staring at my camera lens in their colorful sweaters under the big black umbrellas. The red neck scarves seem to be a school uniform. I guess it represents the 'comrade' concept. I have noticed the children are dressed so colorfully, while the adults are garbed in a bland, repetitious style. The girls giggle and, after my photo moment, they rush on to school. Joan and I follow behind, and walk inside the school yard. I am curious about the classrooms. I am a teacher so this is fascinating to catch an aspect of Chinese education, even if we are not formally invited. It seems that no one really cares. We peek inside at the blackboards and decorations. The kids look outside at our western faces popping up at the window pane and the teacher scolds them. Joan pulls me away and we quickly jump back out to the street. "We've got to keep a low profile", Joan reminds me. My quip reply: "I didn't even take out my camera. What's the harm?" Joan just opens the guidebook to get back on 'track'. I suppose she's right about not drawing attention, and two western women romping around the school yard could be misinterpreted.

Just outside the school, a man approaches us and speaks English. He tells us he is a tea grower and invites us for tea pointing up the road. We decline because we are supposedly heading in the other direction to find the silk factory. We continue down a few streets following the map in the guidebook, but end up at a dead end and no silk factory. So, we start to look for someone to ask where the silk factory is located by using my dictionary. The first guy happily points in a direction back down the road and motions around the corner to the right. Great, that's easy. We must have missed it. We go back and follow his directions. To no avail; there is no silk factory. We try again by stopping a woman. She points in another direction, and we follow her idea. After several wrong turns, we realize (too late) that we are running in a maze of circles by asking people on the road. Each time, a person acts absolutely sure to give us the right direction with a confident face. Lots of smiles and pointing. No one loses face here with a shrug to signal "I don't know". Three hours later we finally find the mysterious silk factory.

At the gate there is a cardboard sign with a message: "Please book a tour with the Chinese International Travel Service." We are stunned. I tell Joan to wait outside the gate. I walk slowly into the courtyard and then, using the dictionary, explain to the guard that we haven't time to go back to the tourist office. She points to wait outside at the gate. Patiently we wait for a reply. We get the signal to come in. A nice woman explains that we can join a tour in Chinese. We agree and follow the leader behind a group. Even without a translation, it's evident that it's quite a chore to make silk. First, we are led to the painting room. They paint patterns by hand in a dimly lit room with about six people. Next, we proceed to the pattern making room, where there is one woman making punch cards for patterns all by hand! The whole process is new to me. I am wondering, where are the silk-worms? Anyway, I appreciate silk scarves made in the People's Republic of China (PRC) more than ever. If this is how manufacturing is done everywhere in this country, no wonder everyone is wearing the same styles. Any other styles would be too complicated at the rate they were punching those cards to make scarves. It would require a massive tech revolution. Japan and Europe after WWII were lucky to have support to rebuild their industries. I am still not sure why we participated in pumping up our enemies' economies (namely, Germany and Japan). I guess it's kinda like good friends are fine, but to be safe "keep your enemies close." China at the moment is neither friend nor foe. It is quite an effort to be an individual traveler here in China; nothing is easy and not exactly as it seems in the guidebook. I don't exactly know what I was expecting to find on the silk factory tour.

I turn to Joan. "I think in the future, we may not want to waste time on hunting schemes for 'factories' no matter how interesting they may sound. In my opinion, we can stick to the historical landmarks." Joan teases, "I didn't think it was so bad. How else would we have gotten a free tour of the city?" I add, "Very funny, Joan. Next time you can tell me about it, while I hang out watching the sunrise. It will probably be faster and more satisfying." Joan only mimics me: "Ha ha ha, smarty pants. Now let's get going, we have to pack for Shanghai."

4

September 11, 1984

Shanghai tickets in hand, we board the train to our 'destination' after the unexpected detours. According to our guidebook, Shanghai is appealing as a port city, and a far cry from Hong Kong. Hong Kong actually was a group of villages lumped together in our minds around a bay with boats of all sizes competing through the water ways to reach Kowloon, outer islands or the 'New Territories'. The Opium Wars (the first ending in 1842, the second in 1860) were won by the British. The last cessation was a treaty signed by Britain and China in 1898, declaring the Hong Kong area subject to a 99-year lease (at least in theory). No one really knows what is going to happen to Hong Kong after 1997. Basically, it meant that Hong Kong may be Chinese controlled again. Now in 1984 HK is relatively more modern than Shanghai. On the other hand, Hong Kong has never been a hub for intellectual and cultural legacies like Shanghai. Albeit, HK has grown over the last century since the Opium Wars to become a bargain hub of the latest technological gadgets and gold smugglers (how did I know? Rumor in the dorm room was you could make a quick 1000 dollars by shoving bars up your butt to travel to Nepal!). We were on a low budget but that was a bit out of my range of 'risk taking'. Needless to say, I am curious to see Shanghai with my own eyes!

Our Orient express (not so very express) is slowing down. I haven't even gotten a sore leg from the hard seat, yet. I poke Joan, "We're here!" Joan peeks up from our guidebook. "Really, so fast?" Right, after two and half days, she says 'fast'. It was actually a short train ride in comparison to the other one from Canton. We didn't even have time to fill up our mugs with hot water. Swinging bags, babies, bundles, make up the swarm of passengers, in a blur of Blue hue. The pack descends onto the platform that is situated in an out-of-date train station with the familiar scent of sesame seed oil frying up something like pork buns. Everyone seems to be in a big hurry! It's rush hour in all directions, everyone going to an unknown destination. I look up and see the Chinese sign for 'exit'---one of my first Chinese characters I had mastered in Japan. It comes in handy in train stations that are like mole tunnels heading through a complex underground maze. Of course, 'woman' is another vital Chinese icon to memorize if you want to go to the proper toilet! These basic ideograms, that I learned in Japan, are derived from the Chinese language, so I am in luck. I signal Joan, pointing to the huge 'exit' sign. She nods her head which is above the sea of blue worker caps. She is taller than I am so it's easy for her to keep tabs on my movements. We are packed into the crowd with no elbow room, let alone a pinky finger gap to distinguish one human be-ing from another. They say every culture has its own social distancing rules: here there is no space available for any kind of distancing! Who knows what the cultural rule in Mainland China is, but I am guessing it's run for your life to the exits! What is waiting outside, I cannot begin to imagine. I would like to see a TV game show that tries to mimic this obstacle course for prize money. The finish line has about half a million people moving in a block wall formation, pressing against each other to the exit doors. I keep Joan in my peripheral vision while scooting vigorously along with this improvisational choreography; a mob frenzy contact dance. Joan is no stranger to foreign crowds.

Joan back home drives around Mexico, just over the border, with a customized license plate that announces, 'Baja Mama'; kicking up the dust of a Tijuana sunset as it blows off the rear of her VW bug through the crowded streets. She mostly was on the hunt for paintings that she could hang on her wall as part of the collection 'discovered' by Joan. Whenever I visited Joan, she proudly gave me a visual tour of the latest artist she had acquired. Her house became a makeshift gallery that revealed a bit of Joan's private fantasy world. Her husband, Paul, never really interfered with her interior design; he was more fixated on taking the dogs out for a run on the beach and catching a few waves with his boogie board. Joan was intent on adding décor to the massive wall spaces that seemed endless to the ceiling. These two bodies in the universe revolving in their own orbits. I listened to her ideas and at the same time was delighted to tag along with her husband to the beach (I'm a boogie board enthusiast, too!). Joan would finally cave in and drive us down to the beach. As we plunged into the icy Pacific waves like teenagers, Joan would watch from the shore on a blanket; coaxing the dogs to jump in with Paul and I.

Anyway, right now she is coaxing me to sit down. Joan stops, or should I say tries to stop. The brash crowd is pushing her along up to the bus stop, where there is a bench. She ducks and covers her head with a swift move to sit. I'm just behind her now catching my breath. People are spreading out in all directions. What a relief! Now what? Joan is holding onto her minuscule space on the bench until I arrive. She pats her lap. "Wanna sit?" I laugh loudly. "Right on, Baja Mama". She is worried about her passport and money. I am worried about our next maneuver to the hotel. 'Off the Beaten Track' recommends a hotel on the river and a taxi (the guidebook recommends spending the money, as it's well worth it!). Dorm room beds are cheap and a good place to swap information with individual backpackers like us. It boasts about the Peace Hotel down the street that has a jazz band in the lobby leftover from the 1940's. I can dig it alright!

A taxi driver approaches us, and I point to our destination in the book. He seems very keen and friendly. But he's not picking up our bags. I get it--- men and women are considered 'comrades', so there is no difference! We lug our bags into the trunk, noting how minimal customer service is here and no tips are welcomed. I wonder if the car is an antique remake or just a leftover edition from before the revolution. We slide into the back seat and hope for the best. The 1940's taxi stops at one of the only high-rise buildings on the block (I figure it has10 stories). It is on Nanjing Road with a picturesque promenade. Getting here is too easy, what's the glitch? We were on guard for the "meiyo" chorus line. I wonder where the dorm room is located; in the basement? The receptionist is ready for us with a smile and kindly takes our money for 2 dorm beds. Joan and I are flabbergasted. Just like that? You ask for a bed and you get it? I nodded with "She-She". Thank you, Lord! We are going to get settled into our backpacker haven before sundown!

We are directed to the elevator to find our dorm beds. Surprise! We lucked out, the dorm room is actually the penthouse. Shanghai is beginning to feel like home sweet home with a few backpackers shuffling through their extraneous pouches and noisy plastic bags. There is nothing worse than someone fumbling with their crinkly plastic bag at 5 a.m. to catch a bus, train or plane. No numbers on the beds, so I guess it's first come first bunk. Since it's late afternoon most everyone is out exploring, so we settle our bags next to two adjacent beds (more like army cots) that look empty. I lay out my plastic rain poncho (keeps the bed bugs out) and my sleeping sheet. I throw the government blanket issued by reception on top and slide my backpack under it to conceal my meager belongings.

We peer out the window down on the road. Joan remarks, "it looks pretty busy and crowded, I hope we don't get lost". I casually calm her down by saying, "Joan, there are hardly any hotels and almost no high-rise buildings. We surely can find our way back from the labyrinth of one-story buildings." She looks up and down the road. "You're right. We are pretty high up. I only see the one across the street that's slightly similar." Don't get me wrong, the streets of Shanghai are crazy crowded with at least 8 lanes of bicycles in both directions and buses weaving in and out of their circular pattern to avoid killing any bicyclist! It looks daring and fun, like a Disneyland ride. I can't wait to rent a bike and try it tomorrow! Joan declines because she has challenges riding a bike (she lost her sense of balance after a brain tumor was removed a couple of years ago). It's the reason she has absolutely nothing to lose and wants to live life to the fullest! I just found out about the brain deal in

Hong Kong! She confesses that she is fine walking but needs a little bit more help in some situations. I don't mind. After all, what was I going to say? We have big plans and no one is going to stop us now! So, she tells me, "I'll stick around the hotel in the morning, while you stick your neck out on the bicycle Indy (Indianapolis) 500 racetrack". Well, that is the deal with my traveling partner. We have agreed to split up during the day to cover more ground and report back to each other. Joan suggests, "We can meet up for lunch". Now that we've got our plan for tomorrow, I suggest we get out and take a leisurely stroll considering we've been running around all day working up an appetite.

I wash my face and Joan asks me if I want to check out the jazz band at the Peace Hotel. Sounds good to me. Our map from the guidebook is pretty basic, but it can't be too hard to find. As soon as we get outside and cross the street, Joan jabs me. I look up at the art deco Parisian sign posted vertically. In clear letters it reads "Peace Hotel". Joan blurts out, "Charlie Chaplin stayed here!" Slowly strolling into the lobby, lo and behold, a cool swing beat is reverberating. I turn to Joan. "Guess we are in the right place." The 'Old Jazz Band' is all decked out in tuxedos in broad daylight. I am surprised. No Mao blue collar jazz band? I am guessing we are in another tourist no-fly zone like West Lake. Joan whispers, "This is where all the bigwig diplomats stay." I can see why, considering its location. It's right on the Huangpu River that empties into the Shanghai port facing the Yellow Sea. We sit down and order a drink to listen to the band. At a break, we talk to the bass player. He tells us that he learned to play jazz in university in 1948!

Now where to eat an early supper? How exciting to be right in the middle of 11 million people (about twice the population of Arizona), but I am ready to relax sitting down at an open café on the river!! We dine at a fairly crowded restaurant full of Chinese (no wonder, given tourism is scant), but the menus are translated into English. How bizarre! I am wishing it wasn't translated. Joan is giggling and reading the list of first courses aloud: "Ginger pig's ear with sauteed fatty rind, fish stomach soup." I whisper, "Joan, please read to yourself, I am getting nauseous." I close the menu and look across at the table adjacent to ours. I see scrumptious greens with tasty mushrooms and rainbow-colored rice. Joan comments, "Remember, only cooked foods, no fruit, no ice." It was blistering hot and I could use some ice for my drink. I agree to sip black tea with heaps of sugar. Joan is still browsing like she's shopping for lingerie from a mail order catalog; her eyebrows rising and lowering with a lip sync melody. The waiter arrives, and I point to the people at the table across from us (they are not happy with my pointing gesture; it must be impolite in all cultures). "I would like to order those dishes, 'She-She'." Joan recites a lengthy poem to order her first course, trying to keep a straight face. She is enjoying the absurd descriptions in English and making fun of them like a high school student forced to read Homer aloud. The waiter nods, and hopefully we may get dinner before the moon rises. Dinner was served in a polite manner and we walk back to our hotel like little fat Buddhas. It must have been the rice dish and Joan's six-course massive meal! I lay here on my dorm bed digesting it all, so far.

My first impressions of Shanghai? It's more elegant than Hong Kong, exactly what I read about in the guidebook. Hong Kong is the hub for most of us backpackers and personally I have been familiar with Hong Kong since my first landing in the 'Far East' in 1982. Two years later, Joan and I naturally chose HK as our rendezvous point to embark on this China trip to Canton. Hong Kong is a mix of hustlers and a myriad of business entrepreneurs; a trading hub in Asia with all its flavors spiced up in a melting wok. The HK Chinese are thin, wiry and always in a hurry to bargain for a sale. This time Joan and I stayed in the Chung King Mansion; a backpacker cheap entry point to Hong Kong, and our first true 'dorm room' experience. It's a far cry from the YMCA around the corner. It is located on the 14th floor with an elevator tucked behind seedy shops overrun with gold traders (smugglers) and other unappealing greasy haired men with protruding stomachs from India or Pakistan hanging out watching everyone's moves.

I turn and look at Joan, who is snuggled, sinking in her Shanghai bed (more like an army cot), and my mind wanders. I begin to think about my own mom. No way would she have been able to do this trip on shoddy beds like these. Nevertheless, she would like to hear about the adventures. I rummaged through my backpack for a pen. I begin a long letter to Mom, reporting on the cultural mishaps and wonderful food (without alarming her, of course). Mom loves humor and different cultures; her favorite book is Don Quixote. She said she read it to get in touch with Spanish culture after marrying Dad. Her Italian background in New York had always given her an edge on Dad to a multicultural exposure. Dad seemed to deal with people as they came along, whereas Mom sought out cultural adventure. California was often too boring for a New York city girl like her. Nevertheless, Mom was Mom (worrying about her baby daughter across the globe). Joan and I knew we couldn't report everything to folks back home, or they'd seriously freak out. So, I keep my letter light and informative as Joan had suggested. My deeper thoughts (panic-stricken reflections) are reserved for my diary. Ending my letter to Mom with kisses and hugs, I stuff it into my bag, placing it carefully between my diary pages to preserve its folded pages intact. I am exhausted; hence my diary only gets a few one-liners to remind me of odd facts and figures. I jot down a few lines of poetry to sum up my sensations; my best tool for short and concise emotional release!

5

September 12, 1984

I wake up early with a faint sliver of light coming through the meticulously clean windowpane as I lazily lay on my bed. I ponder on this scene when dawn rides across the sky, a silent wonder. Sometimes, a universal moment like a sunrise quiets the mind no matter where you end up. I slept well after our dinner and my stomach seems to agree with the food here in Mainland China. I turn and look at Joan. She looks serene, sleeping, in our home away from home. As I scan the room, I realize it's actually pretty full. I'm surprised to see more westerners here than I've seen in the whole trip so far. I tiptoe to the window and take a deep breath; the subtle light is appearing from the East. Japan is the furthest island from China, so the Chinese philosopher-poets named Japan "the land of the rising sun". In other words, it translates as origin of the sun from their perspective. China was the center of the universe, too (from their point of view).

Our guidebook says you can try Tai Chi in the park. I sneak downstairs, wave to the receptionist, and step outside. I'm ready to get into the 'flow' of a Tai Chi lesson. Mind you, it's sure to be with millions of people (I'm guessing). Once outside I turn and head to the park, where I hope I can join in this authentic Chinese ancient martial art ritual. Shanghai seems like it never sleeps; bicycle wheels are already churning, carts are lugging heavy loads, and the sun hasn't even shown its full face. There's no way to miss the park, with loudspeakers hanging in the trees like fresh fruit, and an army of quasi uniformity (white

long-sleeved shirts, black slacks), lined up in rows, with graceful movements, everyone in black slippers with red soles. I wish I had brought
my own black slippers that I bought years ago from San Francisco
Chinatown! It would help to be more serious and fit in! Well, now I
know for next time. It's the first time I don't see a group in blue Mao
suits. I do see a black and white choreographed martial art dance swaying from side to side. Most participants appear to be over 70, maybe
100! It's a great way to begin the day, if you have time of course! I
pop into a relatively free space, and that's not an easy move. Nobody
pays attention to me, the lone, awkward westerner juggling knees in
gymnastic swinging motions. Everyone maintains their attention on
their own arms and legs which rise and fall in a wave, much like a flock
of sacred white cranes in unison crossing the sky on the jet stream.
There's no teacher here, there's no leader, only serene faces, bodies in
formation contemplating in the direction of the sunrise over the river;
dictated to by the anonymous voice from the tree branches holding up
speakers. I clumsily follow in my clunky sneakers. Luckily, I had some
Tai Chi lessons in Japan; just enough to fake it.

Suddenly the voice on the speaker stops. We bow to the Sun, and
our day begins in unison together. I'm grateful to this group for my
initiation into the Shanghai sunrise ritual. The crowd disperses and
melts into the urban background. Refreshed, with a little extra energy
in my stride, I head back to the hotel to find Joan and see what she's up
to. As soon as I push open the doors to the lobby, Joan greets me with
a worried face, "Where have you been? I simply say, "Oh me? I've been
out mastering my Tai Chi, and you?" Joan actually looks disheveled and
a bit out of sorts, "I've been looking everywhere for you", she says. I
gently take her arm and walk to the breakfast room. "Come on Joan,
let's get some food in our stomachs and start our next venture." We
sit down to a full western breakfast: toast, butter, jam, eggs and coffee.
This hotel is pretty impressive, even though we're in a time warp from
the 1940s. Feeling brave, I say to Joan, "I'm going to rent a bicycle
and take my chances that I'll return in one piece!" Joan is reading the
guidebook and nods. She's happy to hang around the hotel and walk

along the river. She utters, "I'll meet you back here at noon." Then she reminds me in a serious tone, "Bring your passport around your neck in case you have an accident." I reassure her, "Joan, you know I always wear it, don't worry."

The receptionist is quite happy to rent me a bicycle, and I'm wondering about a lock. She nods her head. "You don't need a lock here, no one's going to steal your bicycle; that's against the law." She adds, "Bicycles are strictly registered and very difficult to obtain." I was thinking bicycles were assigned to everyone, so it seems there are some privileges. Outside, my bicycle is waiting for me at the front door next to a man in a uniform with a cap. I jump on it. "Ready or not, here I come Shanghai" (I say to myself) as the man waves goodbye slightly amused. The road by the river is pretty easy to navigate as I get into the traffic flow which seems like rush hour all the time. I'm naturally dragged into a pace along with perhaps a million other bicyclists on all sides of me. I suppose they're going to work, and now it feels quite natural to move along this Chinese conveyor belt that never stops. It's pretty thrilling to be riding side-by-side in 8 lines across with everyone pedaling at the same pace. On either side of me people are smiling! I have to say this is a novel experience. Back home in Los Angeles we have eight-lane motor highways with road rage, traffic jams, dreaded detours, and carpooling. However, this experience in the open air, flowing together while buses have to yield to us (cyclists); weaving in and out of this massive circulation of bicycles. This is so cool! Let me remind you that all the bicycles here are the same. I suppose they are government issued. I keep up with the sea of bikes like a swimmer in a lap pool. It's actually relaxing and certainly a joy ride! I don't remember how I got back to the hotel, but somehow, I made it in one piece. I return my bicycle to the front door attendant. The receptionist greets me with a sigh of relief and I triumphantly go to the elevator. Well, it's been quite a morning and Joan must have some news for me.

I look around the dorm room and there's Joan on the bed. No one else is here, except a guy with his headphones plugged into his Walkman. Joan peeks up from the guidebook and is relieved to see me. She blurts out, "Hey you made it, good. Ready for lunch?" I quickly wash my face and turn to Joan, "I'm starving, let's go!" "Yeah, I get it. Your generation is always over exercising." Really? "Back home, I would be jogging 5 miles, and then hitting the pool." Joan only comments, "All you kids are the same." What she really meant to say, was that California women are quite distinct from her upbringing; doing everything boys do. I was no different from her two daughters. I concede, "Walking is exercise, right? Let's get cracking."

Joan had already picked out our lunch spot and I didn't have any energy to fight it, so I tagged along like a little kid with her mother. Everywhere we go in Shanghai feels like a football game has just finished and everyone's on the streets milling around to celebrate. That's a joke! Joan brings me up to speed and clarifies, "Shanghai's 24-hour factories never stop. Shifts are 'round the clock'." I get it, the beat goes on and on and on. Although there's constant movement, it never seems like it's rush hour because people don't seem to be in a hurry.

As we are sitting down for lunch Joan announces that we should try to visit the Chinese circus. Wow, that sounds incredible! She remarks in a low voice, "But the tickets from the tourist service are expensive. It says here in the book that if we hang out at the tourist front door, we could be approached to buy discount tickets". Well, I suppose that means me running around looking for black market acrobats who have a spare ticket. Joan emphasizes, "This is a chance of a lifetime! The Chinese circus is famous, we can't miss this!" I take a deep breath. "All right, I give in." I dig into my lunch; I'm famished from all the sports I did this morning! Between bites I inquire, "Tell me where I gotta go." Joan excitedly explains, "We need to get our stamp for Beijing anyway." We found out individual travel meant permits for each place had to be obtained in advance to buy travel tickets. She reminds me, "It's all in the same place. While you're getting our permits inside CITS, I'll wait outside and look for a local to sell us circus tickets." I reluctantly agree, sipping my soup, because Joan looks like a kid in a candy store. How could I refuse? Joan adds, "By the way, let's try again to get a permit to Tibet". She's got me when I'm down and hungry. "Fine, fine, come on, let's finish lunch." Joan points to a rudimentary map in the book and shows me where the CITS office is located. It's quite nearby. She comments, "Hey, how about we go visit the French Quarters on the way back?" Sounds like a full afternoon to me, but first I'm not leaving until I finish my noodles and second course. Shanghai cuisine has a great variety of dishes (spicy, sour, salty, sweet) and God knows when I'll be back!

I walk into the CITS office and Joan stakes out the door for circus ticket sellers. She's talking to herself about the circus under her breath.

After several 'Meiyo' salutes to our Tibet request, I settle for a Beijing permit. I am exhausted from the fight for Tibet, but relieved to be finished. I push open the doors to find Joan. I see Joan right there on point at her stakeout and announce, "Sorry, no Tibet but yes, Beijing." Joan nods and whispers to me, "See that guy over there, he says he's got tickets to the circus for tonight!" Joan pushes me a little bit towards the guy. "Come on, get the tickets". "Really? Right now? What about the French Quarters? Don't you want to take a little break and have a cup of tea and pastries?" She insists, "We can do that later, don't be silly. When are you going to see an authentic Chinese circus?" She's right, this is the place to see the real deal. Tea is secondary at this point.

I'll spare you the details of the ticket seller conversation. Soon, I'm heading down back alleys, turning the corner, a roundabout, fire escapes and upstairs, down the hall, and I slip into an apartment somewhere in the middle of Shanghai where a family is eating lunch. My contact guy offers me black tea. I'm sitting at the table and waiting for my tickets, I hope; or I'm going to be kidnapped and my family will have to pay a ransom! I'm getting nervous waiting, so they offer me some pastries. Actually, the tea cakes look appetizing, better than the fortune cookies back home. I politely smile and accept. The clock is ticking louder than all our heartbeats combined. Needless to say, everyone here is nervous for reasons unknown to each other. It feels like a Mahjong game, where each player is bluffing behind their set of ivory/plastic blocks. I have a Mahjong set at home that I acquired for a birthday gift to play with my best friend Doug (long story why I had it). We did not really understand how to play, but it was a bit like poker with a walled enclosure made out of the blocks. I do remember how I loved the Chinese characters engraved on the blocks. My childhood friend and I made up half the rules and had a great time with the novelty of a new game. My fingertips relished the smoothness of the blocks and bluffing my way through the game was entertaining. I'm now back to the situation at hand after daydreaming in my own private world to calm down. Who knows what the others are thinking. Childhood memories help me stay focused. Finally, a short guy jumps into the room placing two tickets on the table. I don't dare touch my passport and just pull out some money from my pocket. All good! I'm ready to go, and wave to the family of ten slurping their noodles. I wish I had had lunch here instead of rushing out from the restaurant earlier with Joan. This food here looks delicious. My contact guy smiles and we're out the door! Backwards, down the fire escape through the alley around the corner, suddenly we are back at the CITS front door. I'm sure getting a handle on these black-market deals! Lo and behold, Joan is still there looking around like a spy. I grab her arm and say, "Let's go, got 'em".

It's getting a little late, so we decide to take a bus, since we have to get dressed and go to the circus tonight. Joan has been studying the bus routes, so she knows the most direct one back to the hotel. I'm so tired I can hardly stand up. Oh, but that's not necessary, there's so many people on this bus that I am magically being held up. Suddenly there's a gunshot explosion! Too early for fireworks? What is going on? This is not New York! Who's got a gun on this bus? We're so freaked out! We scream. The door opens and everybody piles out. The shattered glass on the curbside scares us! It turns out the bus was just too crowded; the window exploded from lack of air! I'm telling you Shanghai has so many people there's not enough air in the bus to breathe! I guess this is what rush hour feels like! Joan and I seem to be the only ones frazzled. I suppose this happens every day? And I thought L.A. traffic was bad! We are so shaken up that we decide to walk to get some fresh air, (so to speak).

Circus Circus here we come! The tickets are real! We have prime spots, center row seats just high enough to see a panoramic view under the tent in this wildly spontaneous atmosphere. Acrobats are swinging from every direction, and indeed this is spectacular. Then in the next act, chairs are piled up one on top of the other, and, balancing on three legs, it seems like they are about two stories high, and a group of acrobats climb up and hoist the last one up, arms reaching to the sky! Next come the contortionists in gorgeous silk outfits, accompanied by clearly Chinese classical music! The crowd is cheering as the lions jump with the crack of the whip. I'm sure glad we're not on the ground floor! I turn and look at Joan. It was worth all those back alleys to see her totally absorbed in this moment of her life! She was definitely right; when would we ever get to sit side-by-side with all these families smiling with their boys (I rarely see girls) decked out in crisp ironed blue mao suits in this section, rubbing elbows with the local 'comrades'. By the way, it turns out we are part of the circus cause everybody in our vicinity is staring at us. Joan pokes me. "See, aren't we lucky? I don't see any other westerners in this section here." I laugh. "Joan, thank God they didn't ask for any volunteers for the lion tricks. I'd be pointing to you, baby". We sit back for the rest of the performances, including Chinese operettas and stunning costumes; quite a reprieve from the solid blue masses we've been seeing!

6

Tomorrow, we set out for Beijing, leaving behind the southern coastal cities that are relatively close to Hong Kong. I can't tell you how many times I have boarded that Kowloon Ferry wavering along in the bay between the Chinese houseboats. Let's not forget the 'Do not Spit' sign and copper spittoon provided below as you board the ferry. It turns out many Chinese have chronic bronchitis from smoking or breathing coal fumes, or both.

Joan is fast asleep and I am contemplating the unknown territory of China we are about to enter as we head north. With a flashlight, I am reading up on Beijing and destinations further along the way. Now that I think about it, seriously, without that chance meeting with Emilio in a crappy dorm, Joan and I would be so lost. I am glad today I mailed one of those flimsy blue airmail letters to Emilio, cramming the front and back pages with amusing details of our trip so far. I let him know, somehow, I would return his guidebook after our trip; maybe a visit to Italy on my way 'home'. Meanwhile, I let him know he could write to me 'post restante' Hong Kong, which was my temporary address at the moment. I was told you could receive mail at the main post office in any big city via that address, so it will have to be my mode of communication for the time being. I am restless tonight, because from here onwards I am leaving Hong Kong memories behind, as we slip deeper into Mainland China.

September 13, 1984

We wake up early to catch our train and muddle through the crowds at the station. We say goodbye to Shanghai and settle in for our un-express Beijing ride, wedging our hinds into the local woodwork and hurling our bags onto the overhead rack. Joan unpacks a bag of snacks and smirks. "It is going to be a long haul, almost 1,000 Chinese miles and more than 16 hours of butt sores." I nod in agreement and peek into the bag as if it were a 'trick or treat' kind of morning after Hallow-een. God only knows; we may need these crackers, sweets, and bread rolls on our long ride. Joan slaps my hand like a mother and laughter breaks out with the locals beside us on these familiar wooden bleachers; they are enthusiastic as baseball fans behind the home plate. I am ab-sorbing the train carriage whiff of tobacco, rice, pork-fried something. Nearby, babies are bouncing up and down on their mother's knees in the passageway, and already enamel mugs are lining up at the hot water boiler. As for filling up our bellies, Joan and I have decided to eat two meals in the dining car---lunch and supper.

The guidebook explains that Beijing was ransacked by extremist Mao followers against intellectuals, religious dogma and the aristocracy in the name of the 'Cultural Revolution', so there is little to see in terms of tourism. The wave of backlash ripped through Chinese urban centers, forcing many to the countryside for re-education, with devas-tating results. Joan nudges me and, reading aloud, "The once opulent 'Forbidden City' is in shambles. Do not expect to visit many cultural monuments as they are in ruins or demolished." On the upside, Joan continues, "There are bargains for antiques, so be sure to pop into a government thrift store where Ming porcelain is a dime a dozen!" Joan is a happy camper, since she won't have to search back alleys for relics. I am thinking, no one really knows how China will proceed with older generations from the revolution dying out and a new generation filling in the gaps. I am attempting to get a grip on history with Snow's book (*Red Star over China*), even if it's probably not entirely accurate. His insights in 1936 on Beijing (Peking) are a fascinating read as a reference point before Mao had dominated China!

Time for a butt break from the hard seat bleachers. We scoot out and gesture to our new acquaintances that we are headed to the dining car for lunch. Here in the dining car, I am staring out the window at the countryside in slow motion frames, while Joan studies the menu. She suggests the tofu soup as an appetizer, followed by eggplant with garlic and chili, and plum wine. I pick out another couple of dishes on the limited roster and add the Asian staple---rice. This time in the dining car I am fully enjoying my meal with the savory mix of ingredients that astound me with every bite. The hum of the train tracks intermingled with a different Chinese dialect (probably Mandarin) from the two waiters. It is far more pleasing to my western ears (out of the Cantonese range of nine vowel sounds) and puts me at ease. Comforted by the tasty food and melodious Chinese voices, I am actually relaxing and less anxious about arriving in Beijing, even though we are leaving the southern coast. I am beginning to open up to a Chinese immersion with or without adventure. The waiters are smiling at us and Joan signals them to serve tea. One waiter looks at Joan's wedding ring and asks about her husband. How old is your daughter (pointing to me)? Joan plays along and politely gives my age but avoids the "absent husband" inquiry. I am thinking it's better not to explain too much. I change the subject and ask about the cook in an attempt to find out more about the cuisine. What region is this food or cook from? It doesn't taste like Shanghai. He nods and calls to the kitchen. Three people nip over to our table. "They are from Szechuan province." I ask, "Who is the chef?" The waiter grins slightly and waves to all three (two men and a woman). I get it; everything is in teams here. I compliment the group and I suppose the waiter translates. They bow slightly and nod in unison responding, "She She". Joan quickly adds, "She She". They amble back to the kitchen, laughing. No translation necessary.

I am guessing not many western diners speak to the staff. I look around the almost deserted dining car. Five other tables are occupied by westerners who are absorbed in their conversations with minimal interaction with the locals, clicking their cameras, not paying attention to us or the dining staff who are standing at attention in the corner. Those tourists probably are not in the mass hard seat section of the train; most likely in 2nd or 1st class sleepers, given their pristine unwrinkled attire. Joan and I are dressed in basically clean clothes, but we definitely have the backpacker wrinkle fashion statement written all over us. A woman tourist pauses as she passes our table on the way to her cabin. "You Americans? We're British". As if her accent wasn't a dead giveaway. Striking up a conversation, she adds, "Where is your sleeper?" Joan smirks. "Sleeper?" "We are in hard-seat, no sleeper." The woman gasps, "What! Are you sitting in the third class all the way?" Joan and I look puzzled. I nudge the woman. "Wanna see the real China? Follow me." Following me, she calls over her companion, as they lightly step over bags and stop at the doorway. She curiously peeks into the hard seat section. She whispers, "Aren't you afraid? So many Chinese and you are the only two women?" Funny, I hadn't realized that the hard seat section was jam-packed with mostly men. Joan jumps ahead. "Nope, we are just fine, making friends all the way." She takes my hand tenderly. "Come on, we have to finish our poker game. Don't wanna keep them waiting. Cheerio." I turn back and watch the couple scurry back to first class, on the other side of the diner car---the neutral zone.

Hours pass by slowly on this hard seat. I'm thinking, "Are we there yet?" At least it's not the long haul we had from Canton to Shanghai. On this route to Beijing, we pass the time playing poker with our train companions. I'm grateful for my deck of cards that I stuffed into my backpack at the last minute. It almost resembles a saloon with all the smoke that accompanies these train rides. Smoking is bountiful in this crowded wooden carriage; it billows in all directions. I once heard nicotine curbs the appetite. I suppose it works well in poor countries, but these guys look fit and not malnourished. I think they just like tobacco for the flavor.

Back home, smoking has gotten out of hand, causing lung cancer, high blood pressure and shortened life spans. We had to always find shirts with two pockets vs one pocket for my dad, a three-pack-a-day smoker. Before leaving for work, the 3 packs were lined up on the fireplace mantel by the door. Then one day, my dad announces he is not smoking anymore. He is a 'mind over matter' kinda guy. He gave up just like that! No gradual slowdown. He was determined to make a point about his willpower. Right? Good luck with that plan. Believe it or not, he never did smoke again! He said it was a matter of changing his status: "I am not a smoker." Of course, he gained tons of weight and then had to find a diet plan to curb his appetite. I will forever remember the grapefruit ritual my dad carried out before meals to lower his appetite. He made an art of technically cutting each section of the oversized citrus fruit. He took it seriously, like his profession—mechanical engineer (prior to becoming a businessman). Everything came down to a structural analysis for my dad, including the human body functions. He was a big fan of herbal remedies and homeopathic science to cure ailments, rather than surgery. Consequently, salt was eliminated from our diets to help dad with his high blood pressure. I still don't cook with salt and only sweet butter on my popcorn! My mother never stopped smoking. She's too anxious and always on the move. Smoking is a way for her to slow down and relax---a time out strategy. Even though dad quit smoking (cold turkey), no one else in the family followed suit. Large family dinners or long lunches were heavily decorated with full ashtrays. Cigars were a solution for my grandpa, slow and easy smoking. Unlike most of my friends, I love cigar smoke aroma because it seems like 'Grandpa' is nearby. Needless to say, secondhand smoke was part of growing up.

Here on this train to Beijing, the cigarette smoke swirls around the cabin freely; asks no questions, needs no permit to cross borders, and serves to bond us together in a cloud of familiar aromas. These Chinese fellows are happily enjoying their long cigarette drags on this long ride to Beijing. Can't blame them, no diner car to break up the boredom for this hard seat bunch. At least Joan and I can serve as part of the entertainment section.

I pull out my camera and everyone is laughing with me as I set up an impromptu photo shoot. Joan opens the bag of snacks after lunch, which I pick at immediately out of boredom more than hunger, and then a nap on Joan's shoulder before supper. Finally, the long and playful day is sinking into sunset, and Joan announces Beijing is just around the bend. She points to her oversized National Geographic poster map. Our poker partners nod in agreement. The map is in English, but we show them our tickets. It is confirmed, we are close to the finish line.

Who knows what the capital Beijing will bring. Time to get ready to peel our rock-hard butts from the wooden planks. I am hoping for a less chaotic football scrimmage to the exit door. As the train slows down to a turtle pace, people begin ripping their luggage furiously from the racks over our heads. I instinctively protect Joan's head. That's just what we don't need; a head injury and a visit to the local hospital. There is yelling in all kinds of Chinese dialects and people are hopping around like caged birds about to be released. The sea of BLUE pushes and pulls us to the doorway. We step down off the train, swaying with the massive exodus veering to the 'exit'. It's such suspense arriving to the "Capital of China", once off limits to foreigners without a diplomatic escort, and guarded heavily against Chinese rebellions jockeying for power. No wonder the book, *The Art of War* was part of the Chinese scholarly cannon of literature to avoid conflict. However, Mao changed the game by enlisting the masses to take charge of their own destiny (under his leadership of course). Nonetheless, the Cultural Revolution stained the party, and the blame was shifted to Mao's wife and a 'gang of four' from Shanghai installed in the Peace Hotel; hence, Mao's name was kept clean from that messy era. The attempt to destroy religious rites may have gone too far, even for the Chinese who value their ancestors as gods.

I am really curious how the capital looks after the Cultural Revolution (destruction) sweep. Shanghai was pretty much intact, even as we strolled through the French quarters in a 1920's time warp right out of a movie set. I suppose that was deliberate, since the brochures boasted about the communist 'revolution' meetings having their origins in one of those houses. For some reason Shanghai is always the seat of action. According to the guidebook, Beijing, situated in the northeastern part of China, is a completely different story with its historical consolidated pillars of power. The communist transformation of Beijing meant dethroning the red Dragon of dominion and stripping away all its symbols to remind the masses of a 'New Age'. Nothing new in China's 5,000 years of history, given they name their eras/dynasties after rulers such as Tang or Ming, with colors and motifs. This era is a practical China Blue worker theme. Rarely do I see the color red or the image of a dragon anywhere, the ancient cultural emblems of China. Red is reserved for a star pin attached to workers' caps, a student bandana around the neck, or the flag as allegiance to the communist revolution, making China a unique form of blue-collar nationalism.

We easily arrive at the hotel, get a dorm bed, and settle in. Joan wants to visit the Temple of Heaven as the last standing monument in Beijing, and then the thrift shop. I want to visit the Great Wall, an excursion outside the capital. Other than those tourist spots, we will just wing it and meander through the streets. I still want to pass by the 'Forbidden City' and Tiananmen Square, which are "not to be missed" according to our guidebook.

We decide to explore the monuments together and then split off for strolling on our own since the city is safe, with all its guards posted everywhere (we saw this on the way to the hotel). The book warns not to approach locals because they can get into trouble for colluding with foreigners. Spies are everywhere, so we have to be careful rambling through the streets. Joan is more worried about the poor Chinese who may be punished with severe jail time rather than us. Now I am beginning to understand the delicate situation in Beijing. Time to be a typical tourist, more or less. I am listening to Joan who has had ample experience with political upheavals; she was one of the last westerners to leave Iran during the revolution in the 1970's. Her husband was there on a job and she loved her time there with all the archeological treasures. When women and children were being evacuated, she was one of the last ones on the plane. She stayed long enough to witness as much as she could. Nonetheless, she is aware of political dangers and holds the reins here on advice to keep us safe. I am listening to her attentively and yet she seems to take a lot of risks. Go figure. It's late now, time for bed.

September 14, 1984

First day out; the smaller streets of Beijing are shocking! We stumble onto a mosque in ruins and suddenly a man with a white cap (Muslim) shows up. Joan is rummaging through the ancient wood carvings scattered on the ground. I find a small one and ask if we can take it as a souvenir. The man nods and takes us inside the inner courtyard. He points to an apparent rubbish pile of even more ancient wood scraps and signals that we are free to choose. Joan goes bonkers! She can't decide what to keep. It's impossible to take a large piece, so we each settle for smaller pieces from the vintage beams. Mine is a delicate dragon carving broken off from a longer piece and worn smooth from centuries of hand polishing. It fits easily into my shoulder bag. I slowly take out my camera, and this sweet man smiles for a photo. It is a moment to remember.

We walk out and get invited to have a cup of tea by a Chinese tourist wandering around the mosque, too. We all sit down at the makeshift café just in front of the rubble ruins. Our table is made of marble with fancy iron legs from the past, maybe the 1930's. I am sipping this tea in the midst of the aftermath of the Cultural Revolution. I wonder how people can practice their religions now, even though much was destroyed in the scouring cultural reform orchestrated by 'Big brother and Big Sister'. Joan suggests we head over to the Temple of Heaven, the traditional Chinese religious monument and more popular than the Muslim minority religion. It was spared or restored. Anyway, people rave about it as a 'must see, not to be missed'. On the main road, I see billboards with space rockets that look like propaganda for China to join the space race; absurd in any country that is struggling to get food on the table and lift itself up from basic poverty. Jobs are not a problem, per se. Here, people of all ages seem to be working. I just passed a man in his 70's hanging out with a scale waiting outside the market. We peek inside the market and roam around innocently. Vendors look bored with few customers, and the food is so nicely displayed. It all looks so fresh! There doesn't seem to be any repetition. Stalls have numbers: Cabbage #147, Eggplant #24, Beans #52 etc. I notice that people are gawking and pointing at us. We laugh and stroll along. I pause and ask for a photo from a vendor. He nods with a smile. The natural light from the ceiling makes it a perfect shot. Maybe tourists don't come here often. Joan and I are exploring, curious to find anything showing the day-to-day life in China.

The Temple of Heaven is majestically atop a flight of circular stairs. The number of pillars and icons are distributed in concentric circles with the number 12 (numerology is important in old Chinese culture). From the outside, this temple is a red domed- structure. However, once we step over the threshold, it is another world inside; colors of paradise and heavenly blue skies with angelic clouds. The circular temple paintings surpass my imagination compared to the dull atmosphere I have become accustomed to seeing. The contrast of the artistic palette against the boring blue mao suits that roam around its corridors is jarring. I am standing at one of the outer doorways, and a grandfather dressed in Mao blue is talking to two children. I smile and ask for a photo. It is precious to capture the generational gap not only between him and the children (dressed freely) but also with a glimpse of the bridge to the inner sanctuary of the temple in the background. Joan's mouth is dropping to the floor. She is also flabbergasted. There are no words to properly describe this moment that truly takes one beyond the earthly plane---to Heaven, I suppose.

Back to reality in the street, we try to cross a Beijing roundabout. A uniformed traffic officers are whistling as bicycles flow endlessly round and round, but we can't figure out how pedestrians get across. I wave to the impeccably dressed officer, who ignores me. After waiting for over 30 minutes, I take a chance and grab Joan's hand. Surely, they will stop for an 'old woman'. Bingo! Everyone stops or swerves to avoid us. The traffic officer is whistling frantically to control the 'flow' and we break the Tao; "Go against the Flow". But it works, and we are escorted to the other side. The officer is not happy and does not want his picture taken, as he waves feverishly for us to move on. Beijing is just not ready for individual tourists considering tour guides transport their clients from place to place in tinted vans.

We leave the main road behind and find manageable streets to stroll back to the hotel for a rest. There are hardly any high-rise buildings compared to Shanghai. I stop at an apple cart. It is a misty day, the light is magical, and the people are kind. They pose for a quick photo and I feel it is a rare moment to capture the simplicity of China in the middle of Beijing. Back at the hotel I run into a vibrant Italian woman and our conversation leads to feminism here in China. She tells me about "The Women's Federation" here in Beijing and some books she had been given about the women's movement. I am totally thrilled by the off chance for a first-hand inside story. I jot down the name of her contact and go back to our room to think about questions for an interview. I inform Joan I'm going to visit the Women's Federation. She is not the least bit interested and insists on a trip to the thrift store. Personally, I can wait for antiques, so I make a compromise. "Okay, let's meet up later for dinner and report back! You take a cab to be safe". Joan smiles. "Alright Miss ERA!" I am not thinking about the Equal Rights Amendment, which is practically a joke now in America, but rather the story I can write.

My journalism days are coming back to me and I'm burning to get an interview with Chinese feminists! I sit down on my bed, and looking out the window, I recall how I first became interested in journalism. It was in middle school around 12 years old when my English teacher offered a special weekend workshop as a field trip. She encouraged a few of us to attend, probably thinking it would be a step towards a career in the future. My buddy Eldon wanted to go as an excuse to spend some time out of our small town. Eldon and I shared a common thread; his family were of recent immigrant background. He, like I, didn't quite fit into the expectations of our classmates, or the small-town attitudes. First, his name stuck out to all of us. Eldon told us his mom didn't know how to pick a name, so she found it in a book of baby names. Second, his haircut was unconventionally long and messy, not like any of the guys in our class. We used to call him "Shep" for sheepdog. Anyway, he was witty, and I used to sit in the back of class with him passing jokes on small pieces of paper. We followed each other all through primary, middle, and high school, not missing a beat---figuring out schemes to get high grades. So, he was going on the field trip, and I felt confident to tag along to my first journalism workshop.

If it hadn't been for the lack of understanding about California's university focus points, I may have taken up journalism as a career. The State college system offered excellent journalism career paths, while the University of California prepared students for academia research, medical school, psychology, political science, or law. My parents were determined to send us to the highest-ranking university system: the UC system. I floundered around in my first years of university and spent loads of time in the library (an old habit from childhood) delving into subjects beyond my courses and walking around the bookshelves. In the end, I did enjoy the research side of academia, but statistics was required for the higher levels ('sadistics' we nicknamed it). I admit it was beyond my reasoning ability. We had to take our professor out to breakfast to get extra classes just to pass! On the other hand, in the English department I excelled in writing. The only thing I knew for sure was my innate ability to write poetry. My first poetry course at university was a breeze getting the highest mark in the class! My professor recommended extra reading to expand my horizons. I began to explore the beat poets and their unconventional rhythm (sidestepping traditional metrics) was effortless to me as a writer. It seemed to come naturally. Mostly, it was due to our extended exposure to Gary Snyder's repertoire and his peers in poetry class. It was more based on wordplay concepts. I loved the dictionary as a source of inspiration. I was too active as a kid to engage in reading novels for fun, but our Webster's dictionary was fascinating to me with its alphabetic tabs and strange words. I would study up for scoring points in Scrabble! Needless to say, I was better at non-fiction than fiction reading, but poetic descriptions were always my weakness to enjoy a writer. I guess that's why I was a fan of Toni Morrison almost immediately when our poetry club introduced me to *Song of Soloman*.

I must say, the UC system offered me a huge leap forward in developing my artistic and research capabilities (stimulating new brain cells and neuron connections never before opened). The courses were full of interestingly updated findings, since our professors were on the cutting edge of research. We were given teaching assistants (grad students) to help out with the chore of teaching. I became much more aligned with my tutors than with the regular students my age (not fitting in per se). So, it made it easy to join a poetry group of grad students to exchange ideas and develop my style.

However, poetry is not a 'career' path. Over the years it has become a part of my soul food and at the most unexpected moment I jot down a poem. I always carry pens with me for that purpose. Meanwhile, the chance to explore law by working as an assistant-secretary in a civil rights firm was offered to me, so I took it. I became proficient in secretarial skills, which we were always encouraged to have as a back-up to make a living in dire straits. It led to political science concepts and debates in feminism mentored by women lawyers. I wrote some articles and term papers on the subject and was praised. Thinking it may be my career, I took the exams for law school. Nonetheless, all the lawyers I knew suggested taking a break after graduation. Actually, logical reasoning isn't my forte and poetic reasoning is much more intuitive to me. Test taking requires less philosophical abstraction and more linear thinking. I failed the entrance exam the first time and wasn't exactly interested in retaking it right away. I jumped at the opportunity to travel overseas to Japan, and now just write home to my feminist friends about the conditions of women. I am not sure about law school anymore. I still like writing, though.

Back to my list of questions for tomorrow's interview. I rummage through my bag and find my favorite pen. My friends back home are gonna love this story! I can submit it to a newsletter later. I could try to ask for an interview with a Chinese woman official, even though I was not a recognized journalist. After all, this is a so-called 'equality' based country and status should not matter; probably more advanced than my own hometown. That is the one thing that has impressed me on the trains, how men treat us as equals, with no flirtatious underpinnings; however, I am not sure if it is due to the revolution or the uniformity. There really isn't any difference between men's and women's apparel, on the surface anyway. Even the kids were wearing clothes of all colors with no 'blue' or 'pink' preassigned standardization. Anyway, I can't wait for the interview and Joan can't wait for the antique store. We step out of the hotel with cheek-to-cheek smiles and head in different directions.

I am greeted by Zhu, an older woman dressed in grey slacks and a long sleeve jacket (power suit, Chinese style). She's about 50 (Joan's age) and speaks perfect English. We sit in an elegant reception room and I begin my impromptu interview. I ask about childcare and working women. She informs me that the 'liberation' (careful not to use 'revolution') had changed many things for women and the laws of China are now equality based. She adds reluctantly, "However, in reality things need improvement." She relates that there is state subsidized childcare in the factories, hospitals, and other workplaces outside the home, which promotes breastfeeding times. In addition, there are neighborhood childcare centers. Equal pay is another story, she admits. Sons-in-law are encouraged to live with the wife's parents, and the "one baby" policy is to liberate women (so she said). She speaks very officially on the gains of the liberation, but at the same time she boldly explains how the Women's Federation office is trying to push for more women's rights; promoting theater in the countryside to help explain the reformed laws of equal inheritance for girls and boys, breaking old traditions. Reluctantly she tells me that people are slow to adapt to these changes and continue to favor boy children. She surprises me by going out on a limb to underscore the issues that the 'liberation' has failed to redress for women. She concludes with, "You have to view China over many years---thousands of years---the 70's was bad, but the 80's are picking up". Her English sometimes astounds me, as she uses very up to date expressions. We spend an enjoyable hour together, and I leave with two small books and a couple of magazines!

Back at the hotel, I leaf through the books---Women in Chinese Folklore and When They were Young. I am impressed with the fascinating selection to give a foreigner. On one hand, the modern struggle of women in the movement of socialism in China, and on the other hand women protagonists in Chinese folklore from traditional stories. Joan walks in and is bubbling with overjoy. She can't stop talking and wants me to go back with her to see all the antiques! I try to share my enthusiasm of the interview but she's not in the mood. I shift to the next move and agree to tag along to the thrift store. I probably should pick up something authentic for my mom. She would never forgive me if I didn't. Before we go, Joan reminds me to make sure we get our permits for the Great Wall and Inner Mongolia. I am a bit taken aback. "What? Mongolia? Who said we were going to Mongolia? Isn't that a bit far out of the way?" Joan explains, "Look here at the map. Actually, it's quite close and we only have to stay overnight in Datong, where there are Buddhist temples carved into mountain caves---the end of the silk route." I am astonished. "Wow, that's cool." Joan adds, "In Mongolia, we can stay in a yurt and have real Mongolian cuisine! We are much closer to Mongolia than you will ever be in your life!" She's right. When am I coming back this way again? Why not? Joan reads: "The Great Wall was built to keep out the invaders from Mongolia. The grasslands are immensely open, and you can see forever." I give in. "Okay, makes sense. How can we see the Great Wall without Mongolia and the grasslands?" Joan reminds me, "Don't forget to ask for Tibet." Oh, of course, how could I forget? Every time I go to the permit office, I ask for Tibet. It's a standing joke asking for a Tibet permit that always ends up with a "Meiyo", but it makes Joan happy to try.

When we enter the official government thrift shop (confiscated antiques from the Cultural Revolution ransacking of high-class homes), Joan walks around the shop like a regular customer. Apparently, she made some friends yesterday (friendly smiles in all directions). I ponder the glass cabinets and contents that were once valued in this country and are now on bargain sale to foreigners. It's amazing how many devastating effects wars can have on cultural artifacts! Joan shows me a quaint teacup (Ming) and encourages me to buy it, since it's small and a great deal! I point to it and the young attendant opens the case to show me up close. It is magnificent and I'm sure mom will love it. Now something for myself. I see a special bamboo bracelet that seems ancient and yet simple. I ask to try it on. It is smooth from years of care and I like the way it feels on my wrist. I have small bones, so it easily slips on like it was made for me. I could wear this and it's not heavy---perfect for a backpacker (in case I have to dress up). We head to the cashier and pay. It truly is a bargain! Now I have two rare items from China. As we walk away, I notice Joan forgot her Time magazine on the counter. I whisper to her and she signals me to keep on walking. Once outside she bends down and says, "I let them have it. Maybe they want to see the outside world." I am thinking about how strategic Joan carries herself in the midst of 'Big Brother and Sister'.

Joan already has seen the Forbidden City, so I take off by myself while she hails a cab back to the hotel. She wants to wrap up her antiques to send by post. I dread the post office fiasco, but Beijing is a reliable place to send a box home. I slowly approach Tiananmen Square, a large, abandoned dirt courtyard with a humongous stone monument of farmers (men and women) carrying rice stalks on their shoulders in a marching row. It is quite a statement! In the background hangs an oversized portrait of Mao as the 'father figure' of the revolution (liberation), dressed in the typical BLUE worker garb with his cap. Yesterday, someone told me that bicycles are won in lotteries and clothes are rationed. Extra clothes are a bonus and I see a few variations of slacks and white long sleeve shirts/blouses around urban centers. I don't understand the system yet, but it seems there is a transition slowly taking effect. All in all, the majority of people are still swimming a blue sea of workers dressed just like this portrait of Mao. The square is enormous and practically empty except for a few bicycles and even fewer pedestrians. Maybe they use it for some festivals or special markets on holidays. Right now, I am one of ten people strolling around aimlessly. I do not see any tourists. I pause and take out Snow's book and read the biography more carefully. Snow, the author, was an American, but left Peking to seek an interview with Mao. He died in 1972. On the first page of his book, he describes his departure from the Forbidden City: "...glittering roofs of palaces...in cool gardens...impossible to believe in the China of breaking toil, starvation, revolution, foreign invasion...well-fed foreigners could live in their own never-never land of whiskey and soda, polo, tennis, and gossip, happily unaware of the pulse of humanity outside the great city's silent, insulating walls---". Snow heard youth shouting, 'Resist Japan! Reject the demands of Japanese Imperialism for the separation of North China from the South'.

I walk over to the 'Forbidden City' that once was an elite protected walled compound built for past emperors, bureaucrats, politicians or kings with an intricate maze of living quarters; now in decay without a trace of its previous state. I amble up the front door entrance ramp and notice a mop drying out; hanging over a wall and dripping greyish water on the dusty dirt. I peer inside just over the threshold and step into an abandoned courtyard with weeds and rubble in the corner. A guard in shabby clothes is standing at the side. He doesn't seem to care about me, so I continue to wander around by myself. There is no sense of purpose in these long walkways and empty rooms. Faded red painted wood stripped of its opulence with the passage of time, combined with the dryness of the floorboards creaking here and there, presents a rather ghostly sense. Who knows what went on here in the past? I get the feeling the current government policy is to let it rot and fade into the sunset without any shedding of tears. It must serve as a symbol to attest to the conquering of the Dragon, otherwise it would have been demolished like the rest of Chinese cultural sites. It's a mystery to me that it is still standing. I silently peer in and out of chambers along the immensely long hallways. It is a strange self-guided tour with no signs, no brochures, no markers of time. I quietly nod to the guards on duty at each juncture. I am not in the mood for conversation. Like any elite ruler of any country, this 'Forbidden City' isolated the Chinese heads of state from the world (their subjects) so they could live without witnessing any turmoil or suffering outside. Now it is a solitary confinement of bygone memories with only slivers of light that rarely sneak in from the sky. I ponder how it ever was possible for Mao to overcome this fortress of power that once dominated China. I walk through the same porthole that I entered and once again glance at the portrait of Mao in typical attire that stares at you in broad daylight, just another day in 1984. It's like I am stepping out of a chapter of Orwell.

What's next? I go over to CITS to book our tour to the Great Wall, another notch on the wheel of power struggles in ancient Chinese history. Joan will be disappointed; no tour for foreigners available. I was told we could take a bus with local Chinese tourists. No big deal, I am getting used to the Chinese style of cramming and yelling. It will be a 'tour de force' to get a seat on that bus to the Great Wall. We'd better arrive early at the meeting point. I hope I understood the time and place right, since the woman did not speak fluent English. I've gotta study more! Nonetheless, I learned 'Ni Hou' today---How are you? But that doesn't really help to chat on the buses or trains. I am guessing that Joan will be happy with a local Great Wall adventure rather than a stuffy tour for foreigners. I look back as the sun is lowering on Tiananmen Square.

7

Today we are sitting on a packed bus heading to the Great Wall along with a variety of local Chinese tourists (folks from around China). I am catching up on the history before we arrive. The building of this military defense wall was intended to keep the Mongol tribes from invading China. A mere 21,000 km (13,000 miles) would be like a wall across the Canadian border (5,500 miles+) ---insane! It took years for the Chinese Great Wall to be complete, or, shall we say, to stop being built; 9 dynasties and 2,300 years of construction (older than Jesus, amen!). A long and winding project that even Roman Emperor Hadrian tried in Britain could not compare (80 Roman miles). They say it is the only structure visible from the moon. Its massiveness was achieved by great human suffering and has been the inspiration for many sad ballads. These songs describe young lads destined to be stationed at the 'wall', leaving behind their lovers or families to dig, carve and carry the 'great stones' for a never-ending concoction of military prowess. Rumors say that the bones of those who died while on duty were incorporated into the structure.

I suddenly remember a story in my newly acquired book on Chinese Folklore and turn to the chapter, *Seeking Her Husband at the Great Wall*. It begins, "More than two thousand years ago, China came under the rule of the first Emperor Shihuang. This emperor was exceedingly cruel to his subjects, forcing people from every part of the country to serve in the construction of the Great Wall on the northern frontiers to protect his empire." The story is enthralling, retracing the footsteps of a heartbroken wife (Meng Jiangnu) who travels over mountains, rivers, and snow seeking her husband who was sent to the Great Wall to work as a slave. He is not mentioned as a convict, but rather a dutiful husband (Wan Xiliang) who was taken away by force. Meng Jiangnu wants to deliver warm clothes and shoes to her husband to comfort him. Finally, when she reaches the Great Wall, she is told her husband had died long ago from the "unbearably hard work, and his body lay under the Great Wall." Upon hearing this sad and tragic news, Meng Jiangnu fainted, and builders tried to revive her. When she regains consciousness, "she bursts into tears and for several days on end, continued to cry distressingly. So deep was her grief, that many of the toilers were moved and wept with her." Then as if from a sign from heaven, a length of over two hundred miles of the Great Wall "crumbled to the ground...whirling stones into the air as a violent storm set in." The story has ancient wood cut reproductions provided by the Chinese Research Institute of Fine Arts. The reprints at the end of the chapter depict parts of the story including the skeleton of her husband revealed after the Great Wall collapsed. So, I guess there are legends that back up this concept of bones buried beneath the Great Wall. The story ends with an ingenious plan to trap the emperor into giving her husband a royal funeral if she agreed to be his concubine. After Meng Jiangnu saw her husband properly buried, she jumped into the river and legend says, "she turned into a beautiful, silvery fish that swam gracefully out of sight, deep down into the green-blue waters." Not even the emperor and all his attendants could catch her. I am heartbroken reading this description and I look up from my book, taking a glimpse at the faces around me. The expressions of this group are dull, unlike Joan's excited anticipation. I suppose if we were on an English-speaking tour, it would be a whole different experience. Joan is looking out the window, eager to view one of the 'Wonders of the World'. I can only wonder what's going through the heads of these local Chinese travelers.

The bus stops and we all shuffle off to find our own way to the 'Great Wall'. Joan and I are following along, with gigantic Chinese tiger sculptures lining the walkway staring down on us. We haven't got a clue as to their meaning! I suppose these are guardians, since I don't see any Chinese authorities around. The tree lined path, rather than a busy street, is a nice touch to help a tourist relax with the continuous stream of people coming and going to this monument. At the end of the stroll, there is a lookout point. I can see the endless wall stretched out before us over hilly terrain. We continue to follow our comrade Chinese tourists and arrive at a crumbling pile of stones; situating us on top of the wall. This is a wide thoroughfare with towers every so often that I suppose horses or armies could patrol easily. I bend down and pick up a piece of stone from a pile of shards. It's jagged and feels like sandstone---laden with memories. I am emotionally moved, while Joan clicks a photo with my camera.

Watching Joan, who is enthralled with this monument, brings back memories of my own mother. Although she was busy with her new life (too much to explain), Mom would have liked this part of the trip. Her love for cultural anthropology would have ignited her curiosity. When Mom went back to school to get her university degree, she had been introduced to a whole new branch of studies that opened up her awareness of cultures beyond her life experiences. Her own childhood in Brooklyn had been a bit isolated with Italian speaking relatives, neighborhoods, and cuisine. She used to tell me about sneaking up to the Irish baby carriages from the other side of the street, just to take a peek at those novel faces and red hair! Back then, every culture had its territory in Flatbush: Irish on one side, Italians on the other, and the Jewish upstairs. When she moved to California, my mom had a lot of adjusting to do with such a mix of cultures intermingled together. It came down to Catholic lines, not necessarily Italians (few and far between in southern California) to marry according to her parents. My dad was Spanish and Catholic, which made him a candidate.

However, at university Mom was learning from her textbooks that the world was much wider in terms of religions with very little differences on the core level. She felt akin to American indigenous cultures and Buddhism. She viewed them as equally valid in comparison to Catholics or Christians. My own university years were bordering on agnostic, as a result of fixating on feminists that argued against Christianity. Unlike her, it meant I was drifting away from any system of belief in a God. Mom was relieved I had found Buddhism in Japan and encouraged me (hoping I'd not become a full-fledged atheist) to practice it and reminded me that she welcomed any religion. I remember how she took us to different religious events when we were young to expose us to cultural diversity. I gotta hand it to her for going outside the box. Nobody else's mom was dragging them around to synagogues, temples, museums or events to teach their children to be open to a broad cultural spectrum. Let's face it, she was a grown woman (late 30's) by the time she was attending those college classes and had a clear belief system but was willing to understand other perspectives.

Mom didn't care how long it took her to finish her degree; one course a semester: Introduction to Cultural Anthropology, World Religions, English Literature. She was popular with the other students in their 20's because she would bake chocolate brownies and pass them around class. She never stopped attending college courses even though life interrupted her many times (over 25 years). Timing was good for her, since California was luckily opening up the avenues for women to go back to school; especially for those that had been busy raising children with no opportunity to pursue higher education.

University was a dream to her since high school; she had taken college prep courses, not secretarial skills. To her surprise, she was destined to be married by 18, while her brother was bound for college. She accommodated her parents' wishes and did get married at the designated time. Shortly after marriage, she was supposed to get a job as a secretary like her other married peers to help support their husbands in university. Oops, she was useless. She did not know how to type! My father freaked out! He had to take on extra drafting jobs to make ends meet. I see now why the university degree for both girls and boys in our family was essential. My mom probably sold it to my father as 'a guarantee that us girls could support ourselves no matter what happened'. Needless to say, we were not really given much direction with professions as girls; teacher careers were considered dignified for us.

Bless her heart, she made sure we all had a chance for a higher education by saving money, watching over our homework time, and posting our report cards on the refrigerator as a reward to make us proud of our own accomplishments. It all added up in the end, all her children graduating from the best university in California. She would have loved to be here with me, right now. I was wishing she were in this photo, too. Mind you, my mom likes her comfortable seats (back problems) on any trip and ultra hygiene as a result of growing up in poor, crowded New York! Mom would never have been able to travel like Joan on this backpacker trail.

I am jolted back into reality as Joan extends her hand to help me get up from my Great Wall pose for the camera. I stand up and we begin to walk along the 'Great Wall' that just goes on and on forever. Could I walk to the Silk Road from here? The sun is shining overhead and there are few clouds in the sky. Everything is clear except the silent voices of the masons who gave their lives to this monumental endeavor, similar to the cathedral or temple builders of any civilization around the globe. There is a small sign paying homage to the workers who gave their lives to the 'Great Wall', but the English is pretty shoddy. Well, at least there is some acknowledgment of their effort.

As we climb down and stand in the shadows of an archway, I notice an older woman dressed in a blue mao suit. She's leaning up against the wall and staring out into the horizon. What does this wall mean to Chinese people? I watched this woman for a while before asking (in sign language with my camera in full view) if I could take a picture. She nodded gently and continued to just bear witness to the wall. I did not linger there as I thought she deserved her own privacy to absorb the essence of the experience. Joan was far ahead of me getting some exercise, walking at a brisk pace. I, on the other hand, was trying to grasp the whole idea of centuries that China was entangled in wars and the desperate need to build such a defense.

We pick up our box lunch (included in the excursion) and straddle a rock next to the bus like the other tourists in our group, nibbling on our lunch. It is delicious! It's so refreshing to always get a fresh meal no matter where we end up. No fast food here unless it's a bowl of soup on the corner of a street, which is quite rare to see here in Mainland China. These box lunches are plentiful, with rice and all kinds of veggies and fried balls (contents unknown). Soon the driver is waving for us to board. I duck into a bathroom and then back to my seat next to Joan. The sun is crossing the sky and as we settle into the ride back to Beijing, I am still contemplating what we just experienced on the 'wall'. Joan reminds me that I still have to go to the CITS for our permits to Datong and Mongolia. We are planning our last destinations in the north with the idea of heading down to Xian (former capital of China). For the time being we can use Beijing as our hub to rest after Mongolia.

As we arrive back at the hotel, we are immediately confronted by a bustling amongst the foreigners; we are given news of an imposed foreigner evacuation from Beijing! What's up? Joan nudges me, confused. I approach my Italian friend and she informs us that the government wants everyone (westerners) out of the capital because they are preparing for the huge celebration of the 'revolution' with a military parade. We have 3 days to get out! Well, that definitely changes our plans to come back to Beijing after Mongolia. We are told we need to get our permits in order and pack our bags. As always, there are a couple daredevils that say they are going to hide out and stay. Joan advises us to get moving and I agree.

I wake up early and head to the CITS for our permits. We started with only a few cities on our original visa application. As we go along, we have to add destinations that seem interesting. We are mapping out our itinerary for Mongolia (grasslands) and Datong (impressive Buddhist caves), our added destinations at this point. It seems that according to the trains routes we must first go to Datong, then to Mongolia. However, we are forced to go back to Datong before heading down to Xian. There is no way to go from Mongolia to Xian. It's gonna be long train rides, so I hurry to the station to book sleepers from Datong to Xian. Joan says we had better splurge on sleepers because there are no tourist hotels in those parts. Mongolia is an overnight excursion with a night in a yurt in the middle of the grasslands. I wait in line with all the foreigners who are forced to leave Beijing like us. We are all trading rumors and it's feeling a bit scary. Corners are filling up with military uniforms (green mao suites) on the streets---rifles hanging off their shoulders. Up until this point there were only small pistols barely visible on the police, but now there is a noticeable military presence in the Capital. A western guy in front of me jabbers about getting permits to anywhere outside Beijing. He reports, "My friend just got a pass to Tibet, since they just want us to leave". My mouth drops, "Really?" I get to the counter and ask for all our destinations and add Tibet at the end. The official quickly stamps all my requests and Tibet, too! I happily stroll out and figure, who wants to stick around for a military parade anyway? We got TIBET! Joan is going to flip out. She has been a bit worried about all the military around Beijing.

I tiptoe into our room and sneak up on Joan. I flash our permits in front of her eyes. She is packing frantically and waves me away. I grab her arm. "Wait a second. Look what we got." She doesn't stop for anything. I blurt out, "We're going to TIBET! We gotta book a flight!" She stops dead. "Are you kidding?" "NOPE, they want us out, anywhere but here. So, we got a permit for TIBET!" Joan almost has tears in her eyes. She pauses and stares at the permits. "Hey, that's great! Good job!" We've got 2 days left to arrange the trains, planes, and buses. We are in the fast lane packing and dividing up tasks to make it out on time. The slow pace of China that has kept us lingering on the streets with no real rush to destinations, is suddenly accelerated to join the traffic in the fast lane.

The last day arrives, and we have all our arrangements in order. We bid farewell to our fellow travelers who are headed in all different directions. Our bags are packed, and we ask for a cab to the train station. As we ride through the streets, I notice military uniforms directing traffic. I turn to Joan, who is calm. She's excited with our new itinerary with a permit to Tibet--- no one can complain. As we board the train, there is some kind of problem with a couple Chinese travelers and the authorities arrest them quite aggressively. I haven't been scared yet in China, a little weary of all the authority uniforms, but this time I witness a real issue of policing. No sooner than the 'criminals' are removed from the platform, pushing and shoving is back to usual. Joan winks at me and grabs my arm to wedge our way into the train; we feel right at home with the rest of the local crowd in our usual "hard seat" section. I see the last bit of Beijing pass by through the window. I am turning another page of my Chinese diary; Beijing is slowly disappearing behind us, and we are heading into the northern territories beyond the capital.

8

September 23,1984

We arrive in Datong and as we're walking out of the train station, I notice it is completely distinct from other places where we've been in China; it's a small dusty town, far far away. Joan convinced me to come here after she read in our guidebook about visiting the renowned Buddhist caves; it's also one of the only places to get a train to Hohhot to visit Inner Mongolia (last frontier between Russia and China). She had time to read in Beijing, while I was getting all our arrangements settled. I slept most of the way on the train here. I agreed to come here knowing it may be our only opportunity to see this northwestern part of China. Of course, Tibet is really the far west, but has a completely different historical context with the mysterious Lhasa, the capital of Tibetan Buddhism and monks (still practicing despite their leader fled into exile).

Joan is curious about the Buddhist caves on the outskirts of Datong, given they were leftovers from the traditions established to boost Buddhism by various rulers in China, Mongolia, and India. Buddhism in China could be related to the emperor Ming, who had a dream about the Buddha or Mongolian leaders unifying nomadic tribes with Tibetan Buddhism. Nonetheless, King Ashoka from India has been attributed with the original inspiration that spread Buddhism in all directions. King Ashoka's influence was felt inside and outside India. Ashoka, with his conversion to Buddhism, utilized his power in a self-less act for the good of the world. Ashoka was mortified after visiting the last battlefield that secured his control of the subcontinent of India. Legends say that the king witnessed first-hand the devastation of human lives spewed on the battle ground, and this scene made him repent for his violent wars to secure his power---he decided to convert to Buddhism. India never expanded militarily beyond the subcontinent during or after Ashoka's rule. The powerful king used his influence to send Buddhist monks with traders to Asia to promote Buddhism and economic prosperity between nations rather than conquering with military force. As a result, the largest Buddhist temples can be found outside India; to the east in Cambodia (Angkor Wat) and to the south in Indonesia (Borobudur Temple), where Buddhism became a guiding force in those cultures at that time. Note: Cambodia was the center of influence in Southeast Asia and its territory included parts of the current Thailand, Laos, and Vietnam.

Ashoka also established the construction of Buddhist temples along the Silk Road in order to raise funds for all his Buddhist projects; collecting offerings given for blessings from Buddha. Chinese spiritual followers, disappointed with Tao or Confucius leaders, made pilgrimages all the way to India to find the source of rumors about the 'Enlightened One'---the Buddha. Sutras (Buddhist sermons) were brought back to China and painstakingly translated. Buddhism spread out with variations along the way. Shaolin Temple monks practiced martial arts to defend their Buddhist temples. Buddhism in Japan transformed into minimalist Zen and practiced side by side with Japanese Shinto beliefs (animism). Meanwhile, India has remained an Asoka defense-oriented country (if attacked, will defend) with huge complexities living with three major religions. Today India has a population on par with China. I am curious to visit India to compare it to China; considering each country has its own way of dealing with overpopulation, disease, and class struggles. I hear you can never be ready for India because it is so hard to deal with all the poverty and contradictions. No matter what, I want to visit it! How could I miss such a country that has influenced half of Asia? For now, Datong.

We easily get a room in the 'Friendship Hotel' without any hassles and with a friendly welcome! How refreshing! Our guidebook says: "If you get hot running water, you're lucky--- but it's the only place in town." I am so tired after all the running around in Beijing to get out on time. I hit the bed for a short nap. Joan is ready to explore, so she goes to reception to find out about dinner. I couldn't care less and wave my hand as she jaunts out to figure out the rest of the afternoon. The train was less crowded on this route and people were dressed in more layers of clothing. I hadn't really planned on cold weather. In fact, I hadn't even planned beyond a rain poncho considering we left Hong Kong in late summer and the end of rainy season. I've got a sweatshirt, a long-sleeved T-shirt and one pair of thick socks (cotton).

I wake up from my nap and see a note from Joan on top of our guidebook: "Read this chapter on Datong to get you ready for sightseeing." I open the book and begin to read. According to Joan, Datong's majestic past is the reason we are here. She had met a guy in Beijing that had visited Datong and raved about the historic Buddhist caves. He told her that travelers rarely visit this town considering it's too far out of the way; unless you are crazy like us, wanting to cover as much of China as possible in one backpacking trip, and attracted to the most far-out places. Reading at a snail's pace with tired eyes, I find out that Datong was founded 2,000 years ago but did not gain fame until 386 A.D. It became the capital of the Tobas, a non-Han people (Han is the current ruling tribe in China) that reached its pinnacle when it took charge of Northern China for 100 years as the 'Northern Wei Dynasty'. Datong was both the cultural and political center of that leadership. However, due to a shift in location of the capital to Luoyang, further south, it lost its former importance, and was reduced to a mere 'garrison outpost'. Now it's a mining town boasting the last steam locomotive factory in the world. Its past cultural status with over 50,000 artistic figure carvings in the Monastery means that it is still rated as having some of the world's 'greatest religious art'. Is this the unknown 9th wonder of the world? After reading this small synopsis from the book, I can now understand why it feels different here in Datong.

Joan comes back with news about a place to eat and urges me to get up while it's still light out. I am kinda hungry, since we had decided to save money and not eat in the dining car. We hung out with our hard seat companions with box lunches; a real bargain on the pocketbook! Granted there were less delicacies, but it filled the stomach sufficiently. I thought it is good to have a taste at that end of the food chain; third-class worker style. Our buddies were surprised we could eat with chopsticks, and that won us points to really fit in with the masses. I just finished the last lines of the description of Datong: "Food in Datong is to be endured rather than appreciated." Joan grabs her jacket and is waiting impatiently at the door. "Come on. I found out where we can eat." Joan spills the good news: "I talked to a Dutch couple in the lobby, and they gave me a tip on where to get the best food in Datong. This Dutch couple has been here a week traveling back and forth to Mongolia." I perk up. "Okay, I'm coming. Let me slip on my shoes."

I am up, grab my shoulder bag with my camera inside, and pull on a sweatshirt. We walk slowly down the road that is sparsely populated and no comparison to the other cities we've visited. Joan leads the way like a tour guide. I am so exhausted that I easily let myself follow the leader. She is rambling on about the Buddhist caves for tomorrow's excursion. I am thinking I must catch up and read more before we set out. I am quite interested in the caves since it's the way that Buddhism came to Japan from India. China introduced Buddhism to the Japanese indigenous people, who had been dedicated to their nature religion, Shintoism. Today in Japan, they say 'Born a Shinto, die a Buddhist'. Living in Japan gave me a sense of Buddhism without any pressure. People practiced on their own and went to temples on certain occasions. On New Year's Day (1st January) they visit the Shinto temple, then the Buddhist temple. The monks ring the huge, brass bells and people light incense with a bow. They watch the first sunrise and pay homage to their Sun Goddess from a mountain or at the beach. It seemed rather harmonious how the Japanese were able to integrate both religions. I am curious about the legacy of these Chinese Buddhist monks that went all the way to India to hear Buddha. We come back early to the hotel after supper. By the way, the food here in Datong is nothing to write home about, but I guess Buddhists are not keen on eating like gluttons to reach the heavenly plane. On the contrary, they are focused on non-attachment. We are definitely not attached to this Datong cuisine! I'll gladly take a Szechuan dish in the train's diner anytime. I guess I have a long way to go to reach Nirvana.

September 24, 1984

Today our first day waking up in Datong, it seems like ages since we left Beijing. We easily take a bus to the Huayan Monastery, supposedly one of the largest Buddhist temples in China. We pass the Nine Dragon Screen, a Ming Dynasty montage of glossy ceramic tiles. What a shame these cultural legacies are completely 'Off the Beaten Track'. If this is just the appetizer, I can't wait to see the caves! We slowly enter the caverns to soak up the essence of this silent retreat that transports me to another time zone; I am neither in China nor in the material world. We walk around in 'awe' of the immensity of these carvings that are higher than a four-story building! I bend down at the feet of a statue and Joan takes my photo. Then, she stands in front of another statue, while I attempt to capture the bigger picture. She is an insect in comparison to these gigantic stone wonders of art! We meander through the caves speechless, and I put my camera back in my bag. I just wanna be here and memorize this site with my naked eye rather than through a filtered camera lens. I already bought some postcards outside to save me the trouble of documentation. I have decided to experience this trip both with and without the camera. I write a bit in my diary when I am not exhausted and soak up the rest organically with my senses just by 'being here, now'. My photographer friend in Japan warned me not to get carried away with the camera. She recommended I experience everything deeply, as photos will just jog your memory. She was a poet, too, and she understood me well. Joan grabs my arm and pulls me deep inside a small chamber. She points up at the expression on the statue. "What do you think?" I am not sure if the statue is smirking or just doesn't know how to smile. It makes us both giggle. We don't see any westerners in this chamber and we don't want to disturb the Chinese tourists.

We leave the monastery grounds after a long exploration of the cave dwellings of the gods. As we walk to the bus stop, I notice the houses have beautiful wooden windows with flower motifs. I go closer to examine the designs and realize they are paper! The sunlight shines through the paper flowers creating a lovely peaceful essence. I am thinking that's nice, but paper windows in these parts! There has to be a catch. Maybe it's a closed-in porch. We don't have time to linger because the bus only leaves every four hours, and we don't want to miss the next one. Joan yells for me to catch up and she points to the bus that is filling up with passengers. We dash over just in time to board the last bus before lunch. Joan is sitting on the engine hump, and I am standing. I look at her smirking like one of the religious statues in the cave, "Sorry". She waves her hand. "Forget it. It's a short ride." I am lost in thought of the caves. I am mystified by those stone carvings with incredible accuracy in dimension and proportions. The immensity hits me like the Kamakura Buddha in Japan. I am still not fully aware of the meanings of all these icons, but I feel a tremendous peace after our visit. Joan, on the other hand, is combating the dust coming in from the window. She's in the real world. I pull up my yellow bandana (comes in handy) that's wrapped around my neck to bear with the 'wild west' dusty town; reminds me of home in a strange way. In fact, this bandana is one of the few things I have retained from home since I left two and a half years ago.

9

September 25, 1984

We are leaving Datong to head to Hohhot and the grasslands in Mongolia. Just before leaving I walk slowly to window shop along the main road in case there was something special in this town to take back as a souvenir. Suddenly I stop dead in my tracks; I am astonished to see a dusty shop window displaying tiny black, velvet women's shoes for sale. These tiny shoes have to do with a disgusting custom of deforming women's feet; bound tightly to appear small. It seems like it was a guarantee to keep a woman in her place, 'bound' to her home. Here in Datong, I have seen young girls helping their crippled grandmothers who are wearing these tiny shoes, hobbling along the streets. It seems the foot binding tradition has been carrying on longer than I thought. I slowly open the door that has a bell at the top to signal a customer's arrival. The shopkeeper is shocked to see me. I point to the shoes in the window and take out my wallet. He wraps them up and scratches his head looking down at my (giant) feet. I was still wearing my trusty tennis shoes that keep me safe and guarantee I can outrun a money changer or anyone else! Back at the hotel, Joan is packing and I show her my relished token of male chauvinism. She laughs and remarks, "Good find!". She teases me and grabs the left shoe, putting her big toe in it. That is about all that fits in it. She smiles, "I guess it's not for me. You'll have to search for Cinderella down the hall." I carefully pack it with my other Chinese treasures to mail at the next junction. For now, I am dreaming about the grasslands; fresh air, sunshine, open space and a change of cuisine! I am not a big meat eater, but our guidebook plaudits the tasty sauces on the Mongolian meat dishes.

Our launching point is Hohhot, the capital of Inner Mongolia---outer Mongolia is in USSR. Historically, Mongolian tribes were a run-of-the-mill pain in the neck for the Chinese with never-ending wars to prevent them from taking over most of China. Hence, the Great Wall persisted over centuries as a defense mechanism. We are beyond the Great Wall here, so we needn't be pole-vaulting over it. After a hassle at the tour office as usual, we are set to go on a Mongolian tour with a Hong Kong Chinese group. Who knows how we will understand the guide. It's for two nights in a yurt (nomadic tent), Mongolia cuisine (meat, meat, meat-B-B-Q), and whatever else they do in Mongolia. The CITS officer told us it was a 'cultural' tour.

Hohhot (now there's a name I won't forget, since it doesn't sound anything like the rest of China) is fairly large and much more diverse than Datong. I tell Joan I want to go shopping for a coat. What better place to buy warm clothes! We find the government department store that is stocked with a little bit of everything. I look up over the cashier and see down jackets. I poke Joan. "Look at those coats, real down jackets. They look pretty sturdy." Joan agrees. "I bet those are a real bargain." We ask to try one on. It fits perfectly and feels very cozy. There are some wool coats and awesome boots, but Joan reminds me that a down jacket can be stuffed at the bottom of the backpack. She is right. It's as light as a feather or two (more like a thousand I suppose). I am noticing that these local plastic traveling bags have a different motif. Well, I should clarify that statement; they are plaid like all the bags we have seen on the train but with another color sequence. Depending on where you buy your bag, you can be identified by region. Clever for authorities. Here they are green, black and white. Near Hong Kong they are red, blue and pink. I'll get one of those, too. Good for storing souvenirs at the bottom of the backpack and folds up nicely as a spare bag after sending off goods at the post office.

September 26, 1984

Rise and shine, we are up early and raring to go on our 'Grassland' excursion. We can't be late because the tourist office told us the bus waits for no one; a typical warning that is true according to other backpackers, who have missed buses and ended up stuck in the middle of nowhere. I don't doubt those stories, given the low customer service on this 'Off the Beaten Track', or maybe I should call it just 'The Beaten Track' with all the nuisances thrown in for free. As soon as we finish, we can be 'Off' the beat-up track. Don't get me wrong, it's a systematic (bureaucratic) problem, not a problem of the Chinese people. I must say I have had so many wonderful encounters with kindness along the way from ordinary people with smiles on their faces and friendly gestures. I am wondering about the Mongols and the mysterious land of nomads. Europe was almost invaded by the Mongolian armies, but that was a long time ago.

Whew! We made it to the 'unmarked' bus stop. We just kept looking around for a bunch of out of place Chinese dressed in western clothes. Luckily, some of our companions are bilingual (Hong Kong British). They are excited and clicking their cameras more than I am. On the bus, Joan is leaning against the window and I am leaning on her to get a glimpse outside. As soon as we are out of the range of 'civilization', a wide expanse of grassland opens up. There are no words to properly describe this feeling that grabs you by surprise as all you can see are open fields of nothingness; pure infinity. Even in the desert there is a cactus here and there, but here, this landscape is a 'forever-scape'. As the bus stops for a 'Kodak' moment, the crowd cheers and we are all jumping out like Easter rabbits longing for a tasty grass appetizer. The horizon is far beyond reach and blends into the clear blue sky. I love my new down jacket that is perfect for this part of the trip. I turn to Joan. "Good buy!" She laughs. I notice she has a carefree expression that I haven't seen before. I am glad we signed up for this tour. It's good to relax and let a tour guide lead us for a change. The guide is a young woman, quite tall and slim, speaking Chinese and

English. Thank goodness! She is sweet and calmly gathers us together to continue our happy trail. Maybe she is a native of the grasslands and has enjoyed this wonderful freedom of the land since childhood. There is something different about her from other Chinese officials---her expressions, her way of speaking, her mannerisms (elegant).

We get back on the bus for a couple of hours more and finally we reach our destination just before sundown. Destination meaning a group of yurts in the middle of no-man's or no-woman's land. It's authentically nomadic. A group of helpers arrive to assist with luggage and show us our rooms (tents). Joan is excitedly following our helper to our home away from everywhere! Our bleach, white, round yurt is clustered amongst the other ten yurts. Inside, it is a colorful collage of carpets and bedding. There is a wash basin in the corner (don't ask about a shower) and I suppose we will be roughing it for the next couple of days. A cozy den in a place with no boundaries. Joan drops her bag and pulls me to the door (flap). She doesn't want to miss the sunset. I agree and we are joined by most of the group watching our first Mongolian sun going down. This scene of orange, red, and purple streaks across the endless sky baffles us all; even verbose Hong Kong Chinese. We are standing in a hazy stupor cast by nature's beauty, and its universal effect is evident. No one speaks, it is beyond words. In our hearts we all understand, no one is lost in translation.

After the initial bewilderment, cameras begin trying to capture it all. Click, click, click. Sunsets are never the same on film, so I just like to be here in the moment. Joan and I are standing together under an umbrella of a peaceful aura. Joan whispers to me, "Let's wait until the stars come out." Right, I hadn't thought about the night sky! Unfortunately, it's dinner time soon, and our guide is signaling us to get ready. Joan and I look at each other and she smiles. "Did you pack our evening gowns?" I chuckle. "Oh dear, I forgot my pearls." I suppose we should at least brush our teeth and change our blouses. The sky is immensely overtaking us with darkness, and suddenly I like this idea of yurt clusters. It's homey out here under the expanse of the cosmic vastness---feels well protected.

We head into the dining hall tent, where tables are set up for 8. We join a friendly group of younger Chinese. In the center of the table is a large swivel with lots of food dishes (mostly meat), and the walls are decorated in a mirage of wool rugs (looking hand woven) with traditional-style weavings. The place settings are porcelain with silver forks, spoons, and knives. Chopsticks are in wooden cylinders placed on each table. Joan is smiling ear to ear. What a change from Datong! We are really going to have a Mongolian feast! Platters of food, mostly meats, come one after another. Vegetable dishes delicately accompany all courses. I should have fasted in Datong and Beijing. How are we going to fit all this food in our stomachs?! Feels like Thanksgiving and Christmas merged into one colossal dinner! Dessert comes after the endless meal that is as infinite as the grassland horizon. Whoa! Swiftly the servers change into (I am assuming) traditional Mongolian clothes over their Mao BLUE garb, and the show begins! Sipping our tea and dessert wines, we are serenaded with musicians and entertained by male and female dancers! The atmosphere is getting quite lively, and no one is sleepy, even though we just ate enough to hibernate for winter. I am so stuffed and now need a bathroom break. I sneak out between acts.

Once outside, I can hear the music in the background, and I look up at the most stunning starry night of my life! Someone gently joins me. I can't take my eyes off the sky. "It's so gorgeous and beautiful!" She repeats, "Beautiful". I turn to see who it is. It's our tour guide, Sheng Li Ling. She is looking at me, and taps me on the chest, "You, beautiful". I smile back and acknowledge her. "Thank You." I tap on her shoulder and reply similarly. "You beautiful, too". We stand here under a dome of stars for a long while. I am not missing a thing. This star gazing into the infinite universe is enough entertainment for me right now. Back at the feast, Joan is having a good time with our HK buddies, and it seems she didn't miss me a bit. She candidly asks about the bathrooms, "Did you get lost in space? How are they?" I joke back, "Oh I've been to the twilight zone and back. Very basic but nothing shocking." We finish up with a grand finale of dancers and a round of plum wine. Sleeping never came so easily, for I was under a yurt dome, but my imagination was full of the night sky. A run to the bathroom in the middle of the night would be a planetary pleasure ride.

September 27,1984

The next day we are off on little side trips around the area. The Mongolians are famous for their care of animals including horses, camels, and sheep. We pile into the bus and first head to a tourist grassland portrait (shooting) gallery. Our butts are hoisted up on a camel and the photographer shoots his camera. We are told at the end of the trip we will be given our famous Mongolian grassland portrait. It reminds me of a pony show for kids back home. I suppose they opted for camels because it would be unique. This is my first camel mounting experience, and the animal seems pretty calm. Joan is joking around the whole time. She is not used to being on an official tour. I go along with the joke and take pictures of our HK buddies. After last night we are much more familiar with each other. Next stop is the frontier. I am wondering what a guard station is like at the Russian border (outer Mongolia). Everyone is a bit more serious on this part of the ride. We don't see anything for miles. Suddenly the bus stops at a pile of rocks with some flags flapping in the wind. Sheng Li announces that we have arrived at the border. Wow! This is the tiniest border post I've ever seen. There are two young guards in mao green suits with small rifles sitting on the pile of rocks. We walk right up to the rock formation and Sheng Li tells us a story of the separation of Mongolia into Inner and Outer regions. Chinese on one side and Russian on the other side. Mongolia is the buffer zone. OMG, where is the postcard shop? I've gotta have a picture of this site. Who knows when I will be back in Mongolia. We hang out for a bit and then it's back to the yurt hotel for a nap before lunch and dinner.

Our stay in Mongolia has been so much more interesting than expected. I will never forget the night sky and the open, endless grass. In Chinese folklore, there are stories of romantic escapades to the grasslands as a refuge from wartime, passing over to the untouchable frontier. Our guide has told us a few folk tales. My down jacket has been officially broken in with the cold breeze of Mongolia and my palate has new flavors to remember. Joan wanted to bargain for a wool rug in the dining room, but they weren't going to give up their decorations. I told her, "How are we going to carry a Mongolian rug back to the post office?" She had no qualms about dragging it all the way back to Hong Kong if need be. She was even making arrangements to mail it home with one of our new-found friends from HK. She's crazy, but gotta love her for getting off the couch and taking an adventure with no qualms about what her husband says! She told me her husband would never do what we are doing, so she had to make the best of this trip! She did manage to sneak out with a kitchen spoon with a little help from Sheng Li. Bless her heart, she is a great tour guide. I asked her if we could stop one more time before returning to Hohhot to savor the open fields. She made it happen. She whispers to the bus driver and hands him a couple of bills. Sheng Li stands up as the bus stops. "We can stop here for some last photos." She smiles at me, and everyone gladly scampers off the bus as excited as the first time we came across this unique natural beauty. As I step off the bus: "Thank you, Sheng Li. This is really beautiful." She steps down with me. "You beautiful, too." It is midday and the sun is high in the sky as a bird passes overhead; almost heaven here. Joan has the same carefree expression on the way back as on our first encounter with the grasslands. I've got to write to Mom about this excursion. It would have been right up her alley! Unlike Joan, Mom would be joining the dancers and fiddling around the kitchen for recipes. Dear Mom...

10

September 28, 1984

At last, we are going to Xi'an, although it seemed like we would never arrive when we were traveling through the endless landscapes. The Chinese train system is a little lacking for long distance travel--- one station sells tickets for one destination and does not let you buy another ticket for the next destination. If you need to change and don't make a reservation, all you may get at the last moment is a hard sleeper to continue all night. Our plan was to transfer in Taiyuwan from Datong, then book the sleeper (luxury for us) to arrive in Xi'an. What's the point of staying in Taiyuwan? There are no interesting sites there for us. We want to keep going to spend more time in Tibet. Taiyuwan is just a mandatory stopover to get the next ticket to Xi'an.

To our surprise, there is no train tonight to Xi'an, so we reluctantly head to a hotel for the night. Our guidebook says to barter for a dorm room. When we arrive, the kind taxi driver carries our bags and is waiting to carry them upstairs. I inform him it isn't necessary--- knowing as usual it would take an hour to get a room. Trotting off to the reception desk, which I could not find, I run into a western woman. I begin to speak, but she interrupts in Spanish "I don't speak English". I stutter in my broken Spanish, "Where is the reception desk?" She points down the hall and I approach reception with caution ready to bargain for beds. It is 50 Chinese Yuan ($20) for a double room. I decline, "No, we can't afford it, we are kinda like students. Where are the dorms?" The receptionist replies, "No dorms." He notices I'm not moving, so he finally says, "20 Chinese Yuan ($8.00) for a double." I agree. I report back to Joan: "We have a room".

Now, what about dinner? It is already 8 p.m. and Chinese restaurants have strict eating times---so we walk directly to the dining room in the hotel instead of going out. A group is eating dinner and all of them are staring at us and our backpacks. Mind you, they are all dressed in fancy evening clothes. In fact, these are the very same people we had already encountered on the train. Back on the train, they had reserved the entire dining car; ate all the food and drank all the wine. Needless to say, we were sent back with box lunches on our hard seats.

Now here we are again, confronting the challenge of food supplies with this group. The guide in charge comes to us asking if I speak French. My response, "No, Spanish or English?" Soon another guide is summoned who can speak Spanish. My mind is working overtime to remember high school Spanish. I am still not sure why my father never spoke Spanish to us. It must have been some immigrant thing to be 'all American'. The Spanish guide is asking me questions unrelated to dinner---"where are you coming from?" I oblige, waiting for an opening, "Datong". He speaks quickly and I finally get the gist of his instructions; we can have the leftovers of the tour since the kitchen is closed. This hotel is booked for tours so our impromptu arrival (as individual travelers) lands us in a private room but no meals. After we eat sitting in a corner like naughty children, we are taken to our room with excellent service. We try to tip, but are refused. On top of that our room turns out to be first class---a real cushy bed and soft towels! Better than the hard sleeper, by far!

We now have a good rest away from the smoky train cars we had just sat in for the past 6 hours. Sitting on that train from Datong to Taiyuwan, I stared out the window wondering how the people in these parts could live. The soil has nothing to offer for farming but sunflowers? I have never seen such fields of never-ending sunflowers! I do not even like sunflower seeds, and certainly you can't live on them alone! Nonetheless, I was mesmerized by the sea of yellow and the unforgettable span of those giant blossoms across the wide horizon. There was nothing to block the view and I could disappear for a moment from China, the world, hard seats, the tobacco aroma and my sore butt. In between the vast swatches of Van Gogh amber hues, the farmhouses were adobe style and sometimes an oven could be seen in their front yard with children all bundled up in layers of clothes. I could see sunflower stalks pulled up by the roots and drying out, hanging over the wall to dry. I just don't know how poor people before the 'liberation' of 1949 survived in the harsh climates. I sense that people seem to be basically fed and easily amused with a change like us on the train. The hard seats are horrible sometimes, especially at night. Some travelers even have to stand for hours. I don't understand their ration system in handing out seats. Other travelers have soft compartment sleepers— 30-50 Chinese Yuan a night (15-20 dollars). We can't even afford that price. And the tour groups are strange to me---just whizzing through China in soft seats. We got a glimpse of their compartments when we tried to get a hard sleeper.

Anyway, right now in this hotel room, I'm quite content to be on a tiny break from backpacking. I have a huge double bed to myself, and the bedding is first class amazing---so I'll just enjoy it. When I was a kid on vacation, we would stay at the famous low-cost Motel 6; all five of us crammed into one room---two double beds and a roll-a-way. We drove for miles visiting cousins in Nevada and Idaho to get to know our early roots in America. My father's grandfather was a homesteader. He came as part of the wave of immigrants seeking a better future in the early 1900's; he bought a shirt and an axe to build his log cabin. From there he began his ranch in the middle of nowhere. Ten years later, he sent for his family; his wife (a successful dressmaker) and their five children were uprooted from the bustling industrial city in Northern Spain to join him in a place where only hunters would occasionally pass. In the family album, the photos of my father's grandmother are astonishing before and after her immigration from Spain. Their daughter, my grandmother (Abuela), knew how to ride horses and probably round up cattle. Besides ranching skills, her father had insisted on schooling for his children to learn American English, even though he knew British English after being a seaman for British ships. Most likely he crossed the English Channel transporting a high quality of iron ore, in demand, from Spain apt for specific Bessemer processing. It highly contributed to reduced production cost since it eliminated coal from the mix, boosting European industries. It is an enigma why Spain was mostly left out of the industrial revolution, given these mines were so productive. British entrepreneurs were the first to own them, exploit them, and hire ships to transport the ore. However, after Spain seized the mines, through legislature against the British owners, work surely fell off for seamen like her father. Nonetheless, the ranch was no place for his daughter; an unmarried young woman coming of age. After she won the bread making contest in the small nearby town, she worked for the mayor, leaving the ranch behind. Shortly thereafter, she was a traveler herself and escaped to Hollywood inspired by all those movie star magazines of the 1920's; she found a job in Beverly Hills as a cook. She was bilingual and could organize the kitchen help and deal with the suppliers, so she was promoted. I guess it was inevitable the milk-man, my grandfather (Papa), would fall in love with the dressmaker's daughter and she would give up her single life to settle down.

Much like my mother's father (Grandpa) who fell in love with Grandma after singing in the streets to sell his father's vegetables (a peddler) and then eagerly carrying the groceries to her doorstep. He was sternly informed from her mother, that he would only be able to marry her if he settled down with a real job. It prompted Grandpa to sign up to work on the docks in the New York shipyards, (through rain, sleet, snow and blistering heat) proving he could be counted amongst the Longshoremen's Union of steady workers, with a weekly salary. No one could resist Grandma's beautiful eyes and silky long hair, not even the nuns at the Catholic orphanage who refused to cut her hair during her 2-year stay as a child. The judge also recognized Grandma's beauty and talent, when he asked her to come up to his desk to translate for her mother's trial; a pleading woman speaking Italian trying to win back her children after being away in a mental hospital for a nervous break-down (left by her husband with three small children, no English, and only a night shift job scrubbing Wall Street floors). When I look at her photographs, I see a worn-out woman. On the other hand, Grandma was photographed sitting perfectly poised on a stool with a vintage 1920's telephone in her hand, and a playful smile. Style and dress were a significant part of her generation on the cusp of the New York jazz era. She passed on that legacy to my mother. Was it the fashionable gown, my mother begged to borrow from the Montebello dressmaker, that helped my father fall in love and settle down? I would never know, I never asked.

My parents were an odd couple of sorts, one from a matriarchal Italian extended family and the other from a small patriarchal Spanish community. Nevertheless, both had hard working parents who were clear about making each generation better and instilling those values in us. So, we hadn't stayed in luxury hotels growing up, and in lieu of such amenities, our college was assured to be paid with their savings. Right now, I am actually going to soak up this spacious, comfortable hotel room, a well-deserved break. Joan has pretty much the same idea, stretched out on the bed with plenty of room for her long legs.

September 29, 1984

It's going to be a dreary day as I look out the window and see gloomy weather. The train from Taiyuwan to Xi'an is 12 hours; I am dreading the trip since I woke up with a cold. I really wanted to stay one more day in our nice, cushy hotel room, but Joan is ready to go. I took some cold medicine (I never take medicine for a cold), but I think it's best to be fair to Joan to stop my runny nose and sneezing. We are in close quarters on these hard seat trips, so to be congenial I'll swallow the pill.

Joan reads to me from our guidebook as I fade in and out, drowsy from my meds on this train ride to Xi'an. She reckons the city is pretty important considering it played a prominent role in the overall picture of Chinese history. I listen to what seems like a fairytale as she retells me the story. Xi'an was established as the center of China along with the first Emperor of China: Qin Shi Huangdi. To clarify, becoming an emperor in China was based on successful victories (bloodshed, destruction, pillage) over warlords, kingdoms, and smaller independent rulers. Once surrender was accomplished after the wars, leaders were limited in power and pledged allegiance to the new 'Emperor'. A centrally controlled state was established. Some territories were negotiated with more sovereignty, such as the Korean peninsula or Taiwan island to the east, Mongolia to the north, and eastern territories. Let's face it, declaring yourself an emperor was no everyday act. You had to conquer the stubborn feudal lords and unify the vast territory with auspicious signs from Heaven to ensure success. Xi'an became a well-known center for a new era in Chinese history.

I listen quietly as Joan continues dabbling in Chinese history, explaining that the first Chinese empire based in Xi'an was no small-scale operation of a fleeting moment, but rather a long line of successions lasting 1,000 years, and its size was comparable to the Roman empire, if not larger. Over time, Xi'an as a capital of China waned and transitions took place. The Silk Road brought foreigners from the West and Mongolian leaders ruled China with its command on nomadic territories along that trade route. Beijing, located in the northeast of China, became important during the 20th century because of the threats from the east and north, such as the Soviet and Japanese intruders. A long and winding road to navigate Chinese history, not to mention the wives of emperors who vied for power producing potential crown princes (no wonder such emphasis on boys). If a crown prince (heir) was too young to rule after his emperor father's death, his mother became the dominant head of state; a golden widow! All in all, there was no democratic rule and the 'subjects' of these reigning powers (men or women) were tossed from side to side as warriors in the crossfire (no worse than being sent to the gallows in Europe to row your life away at sea). Except, Chinese wars were mainly fought in rivers, valleys, gorges, mountains, or deserts on one continent with heavy armor to protect against the refined, swift sword action. No wonder the Shaolin Temple monks were versed in wielding a sword with all those constant battles!

By some accounts, bribes were later implemented as a way to avoid endless wars; saving money and lives (the art of no war). Definitely a new outlook on corruption to control your friends and foes.

Spain's civil war could have learned this earlier rather than later saving a torn country and even worse---a legacy of family devastations. It was an ideology-based war that split Spanish families and neighbors, which is hardly ever discussed as a dinner table topic. What do you say to your brothers, sisters or cousins who took up arms against you? The battlefields of Spain in the 1930's sent mothers to their tombs crying in agony for their sons and daughters in a never-ending spiral of destruction. How to you respond to a country that had divided their youth, sending them off to bloodshed shared in their own veins? Spain knows the art of no war like a gash cut deep; the wound leaves an ugly scar.

In my family, no one spoke of the Spanish civil war. My father brushed the issue aside, with only the notion that Papa, his father, was set on living an American life where the free market prevailed and he could be an entrepreneur. Papa had come to America and worked on a dairy farm, rounding up cows; he saved his money and became his own boss, a milkman. If he hadn't come to America, he would have been drafted in Spain's wars in Africa (no one ever knew how many years a young man had to serve---minimum 6 years). The Sahara Desert heat may have killed him without ever triggering his rifle, he didn't have a strong constitution. His older brother protected him, and invited him to America. Later, after he married my grandmother he couldn't go back to Spain on the verge of a civil war---he may have had to fight his other brothers. It's always a tragedy fighting a war, but some enemies are easier than others to justify. Spain remains a testimony to the raw violence that war drums that can beat to insane outcomes. Spaniards walk a delicate tightrope to resolve domestic conflicts preferring consensus and even corruption if it avoids war; the art of no war in practice. No one speaks too loudly at their dinner table. I never heard Papa raise his voice, although everyone knew he had the last word. The décor in their living room has an enormous painting over the sofa of a European port depicting a time long ago, a replica of maybe an old,

Spanish master. It creates a serene, nostalgic dreamy atmosphere with its misty waterfront, clipper ships and classic cathedral dome in the background. A time when trains had not yet, even been invented.

The train pulls into Xi'an and even though there are loads of things to see here, Joan and I decide to hit only the main sites due to our unexpected trip to Tibet after this Imperial stopover. Joan feels Tibet is far more worth the time than a couple extra pagodas in Xi'an. However, she definitely does not want to miss the archeological ruins and remnants of the Ming Dynasty (maybe I'll find a matching teacup for my mother). Considering that the Cultural Revolution wiped out historical structures and their functions, our guidebook claims that "the search for monuments is in itself an adventure." Count me in!

September 30, 1984

Our first day here and it is raining and raining. Luckily, we are going to the "Terracotta Warrior" ruins by bus to a make-do museum on site at the archaeological dig. I love the idea of visiting ancient history and this type of figurine is a plus for me given my affinity to ceramics. Everyone tries to get us on a tour; "nice, air-conditioned bus, you see 4 things for 5 Yuan". Anyway, we avoid the tours and head for the local bus armed with one sentence in Chinese given to us from reception at our hotel: "Where's the bus to the terracotta warriors?" Some Chinese guy puts us on the bus. Joan is given a seat next to driver (elder preference) and I am standing up looking straight ahead out the windshield. We get off at our 'stop' and stroll along in the countryside on a path lined with my favorite kind of trees: birch trees with their leaves turning yellow and serene white bark. The rain has stopped and it has turned out to be a pleasant autumn day. I could be anywhere in the world enjoying the fresh smell of rain and these trees that make me feel at home. We enter a concrete compound where there is a museum with glass cases displaying the clay terracotta warriors that were excavated from the tomb. I jot down some notes about Qin Shi Huangdi's mausoleum: 14,260 square miles, 6,000 figurines, 2,200 years ago.

I am astounded as we move pass the room with glass cases and enter the original archeological dig; a magnificent site before our eyes. There is a roof and nothing more. We can walk around the entire site on ramps overlooking the site and peer down at these life-size clay figurines that are finely sculpted and in perfect condition in this room. I am staring at these men (presumably) dressed in armor, no weapons. All their hands are in different positions. Their faces are determined, looking straight ahead, on guard with long hair pulled to the left side. Some have no armor. Horses and warriors all facing out front to guard the emperor. There are thousands under this structure that is the size of a Laker's basketball gymnasium!

I am taken aback and fully appreciate this monumental project, reminiscing about my own experiences in ceramic studios since I was 15 years old. Ceramics has been part of my life wherever I've been (high school, university, Japan). I have fond memories of my first high school ceramic studio and Danish teacher, who spent early mornings and late afternoons loading our masterpieces into the kiln (dangerously high temperature oven). Whenever I went into the ceramic studio, I fell into a peaceful state of mind. It was probably because it was an escape from the demanding college prep courses like chemistry or trigonometry in the middle of a high school day. After school I played badminton, fully engaged in winning with mental strategy and physical stamina! I was a champion in our school club. But in the ceramic studio I entered an unknown territory of playful learning; an anomaly amidst the culturally ambitious society that pushed everyone to the max from age 10 onwards. I think this serene, non-competitive influence was due to our teacher; he was from Denmark and an artist. At least that was my impression from his unique behavior to gently motivate us. I was calm as soon as my hands touched the clay. I usually began by massaging the clay like pastry dough to eliminate air bubbles (if not, it meant exploding pieces in the kiln). Then I would roll it out into a flat slab in a meditative manner to create an even thickness. After that, I cut it with wooden tools that were smooth and lightweight. It was a precise process that no one was rushing you to finish, unlike the exam atmosphere of other courses. Careful steps were needed to create a final piece of artwork, all at your own pace. The potter's wheel was another stage of my ceramic progress. The gentle spin of the wheel and concentration necessary to optimize the centrifugal force to center the chunk of clay was delicate and required a certain amount of finesse. However, we were encouraged to work on hand building apart from the wheel---to open our minds to creative ideas. He arranged excursions to the college across the street to expose us to the latest ceramic artworks. Back in the studio he would encourage me to undertake methods I had seen from the field trip, with a helping hand. I liked recycled glass as it melted in the crevices of the clay after firing. Lace was dipped in wet slippery clay and its texture left behind a unique effect as it burned off in the final process. He was a wonderful mentor and very patient. He was only upset when he found 'vases with holes' (bongs) made by the potheads, which were inappropriate for young high school age artists. No wonder there was no end to volunteers to load the kiln after school! They would try to sneak in a few of their own projects without teacher approval. For me I made innovative plant hangers, mugs and a special cookie jar in high school. My mom loved how I sculpted a lion's face on the cookie jar and she kept it as a memento for years.

In university, even though I wasn't an art major, I always took a ceramics course. By that time, I was up to the advanced levels of ceramics, and we were making our own color glaze recipes, experimenting with film on texture, and clay mixtures in huge mixers. Our professor had prohibited the potter's wheel because he realized that university students were not delving into the 'art' of ceramics with a wheel, but rather taking advantage of the free-of-charge ovens, clay, and glazes (all quite expensive) to sell their pottery at local art markets. I was aligned with the professor in the art of ceramics, hanging out for hours in the university studio creating avant-garde pieces.

To be fair, I had the advantage of popping over to my neighbor's backyard when I was a kid to watch Mrs. Z on the potter's wheel or glazing a garden sculpture. Mrs. Z was a bona fide ceramic artist with her own studio and selling her work. She was a great role model in my childhood. I am sure it was the reason I started ceramics in the first place. Most of my friends were in music or drama classes as elective choices. I sort of gravitated towards ceramics for the solitude aspect and the tactile elements, not to mention getting dirty in the middle of the day at school! In the 1970's, ceramic plates, coffee mugs, hanging planters, and original ceramic pieces were popular thanks to the earth tones and originality that fused with the overall 'back to the Earth' concept. We saw films about the history of ceramics that showed us it was a basic skill for humans to have mastered since civilization began in settlements. It's all about transforming clay and mixing fire elements to solidify its use as decorative or functional.

Right here, these clay soldiers are decorative and uniformly un-glazed (one firing), hence the term 'Terracotta (non-glazed) Warriors'. I am in a daze surrounded by this army of clay. We move on to another section, where the warriors are sunken in the earth, still standing at attention, trapped in time. It's actually quite sad to witness this over-whelming sight. Can't help wondering how many people it took to build and sculpt the whole gargantuan project. The afterlife eludes even the greatest rulers who try to continue their control after death. What's the point in dragging everyone else down in the dirt? Here I am surrounded by a belief that these clay soldiers could protect and assist the long-gone emperor. What a waste of money, let alone the toil of people who had to dedicate their time and energy to this monument. Not surprisingly, there was an agrarian revolt afterwards.

We hang out in Xi'an a couple of days more because National Day is approaching (the reason we had to leave Beijing) and we don't know what is going to happen. During my strolls around the city, I see a sizeable abacus for sale in the window of a shop. It is quite large in comparison to ones we played around with in middle school in math class (1970's). Our teacher, Mr. Chu wanted to explain the ancient counting system of his homeland---China. We were taught how to calculate using the beads on a small abacus he handed out for the day. I remember thinking it was pretty cool to avoid paper and pencil scrib-bling. We were enthusiastic about recycling paper to save trees, since my homeroom teacher had started a paper drive; we stacked up used newspapers from home in the back of the classroom and calculated the number of trees we saved! Of course, I wasn't as cheerful when we had to learn to use the slide rule! What a disaster I was at my first attempts. I had to ask my dad to help me. He was a math genius and has a natural love for numbers. We were scheduled to take college prep courses with advanced math subjects under his advice, not necessarily because we were loving it. My dad on the other hand took all his math and sciences classes because he was fascinated by them. He had no idea about college or university until he found out that his friend (who my dad was tutoring) applied to attend a polytechnical college in Texas. When he asked his counselor in high school if he could go to the same college as his friend, he was surprised (as much as the counselor) that he had all the courses necessary and the grades! Before that moment, he had been training to be a carpenter. (Garfield high school was not exactly encouraging high achievers. In fact, only 3 students went to college from his school---the movie Stand and Deliver is film based on a true story about a physics teacher who motivated his students beyond other teachers' expectations). Dad's skills as a carpenter were superb (precisely measured, sanded to perfection, varnished evenly) and we even kept a record cabinet as a keepsake of his talents in our house. Despite his excellence as a woodworker, he wanted to learn beyond his woodshop classes. He's not one for being stagnant in life, especially when it comes to learning new subjects; photography, wine, cows, microchips, homeopathic medicine. I remember how he studied computer programming with a copy of a book, neatly arranged in a giant binder, sprawled out on the floor in front of the TV news. He was a late bloomer to informatics since his engineering degree was in the 1950's. Computer programming was his new 'hobby' before purchasing a huge computer (size of a room). My dad is a self-taught kinda guy and showed us that concept to survive. Rarely would he tutor me in math or science without turning to the first pages of the book, and make me read them aloud! After a while, I stopped asking for help and just read the chapter silently to myself. As far as his own higher education, he was only missing one subject; a foreign language. Easy enough, he enrolled in Spanish and passed with problem (he was bilingual). This abacus reminds me of him, so I'll send it home as a souvenir.

Nothing happens on National Day; just more people on the streets. In Beijing there was a huge celebration in Tiananmen Square with millions marching towards the square. We see glimpses of it on a T.V. (a rare commodity we haven't seen in other areas) in the hotel. It looks like a peaceful event. Our roommate, Lee, who adopted us from the dorm, couldn't give us any more information about the elusive 'celebration'. He is studying in Beijing and helped translate bits of the report. However, he suggests we go to Ban Po together. Ban Po is a Neolithic village dating back 6,000 years! Lee translates the captions on the signs posted, which in his opinion were socialist propaganda. Over lunch, Lee explains several aspects of China, such as the unit managers called "Danwei", who control people's lives. He remarks, "It's clear we are in 'Red China' no doubt about it" (rather BLUE from where I am sitting). He continues, "Don't forget, it's not a democracy. No free market, no choices, incessive spying on each other". I suspect he's rather disappointed and senses the 'Big Brother - Big Sister' aspect more deeply knowing how to read Chinese and understand conversations. Joan veers away from the subject and pokes fun at lunch, "Where are the fortune cookies? Pass me the teapot".

Tonight, we are all packed and tucked in our beds ready for whatever comes our way! Tomorrow, we will go to Chengdu to fly to the mysterious capital of Tibet, Lhasa, located in the highest mountain range of India and China combined. Luckily, it's a short flight. Better, since I don't exactly trust the Chinese airways. I am lying awake contemplating our unbelievable luck on this whirlwind tour of China, so far. Neither of us has gotten stomach aches, no problems with authorities, and really kind people along the way to explain the inside view, like Lee or Mr. Pam. We met Mr. Pam in Datong, and he took us for dumplings; he remarked that everything was expensive. He talked of his childhood how little girls who could not play---weeping from having their feet bound. These tidbits of life told by a few who dared to talk to us will remain with me forever.

Joan and I are becoming more confident as the trip unfolds. I remember the first day, Joan was scared shitless in the train. After a few hours she got the hang of it. It was priceless when she first took out our playing cards for poker! I gotta hand it to her, she's a brave lady! So, we are going to her dreamland, Tibet. I hope it doesn't disappoint her. Oh well, too late now. We have our stamps and permits so there's no turning back.

11

October 4, 1984

I wake up early for no apparent reason, so to pass the time I read about Xi'an (Sian) in my book, *Red Star Over China*. Snow claims in his book, that the "Red Army's sensational attempt to march from Shansi to the Great Wall was ostensibly to begin a war against Japan for recovery of the lost territories." Snow describes this overzealous plan as a "somewhat quixotic expedition...blocked by Generalissimo Chiang Kai-Shek...but had not prevented patriotic students courting imprisonment or possible death...uttering the forbidden slogans: 'Cease civil war!' 'Cooperate with the Communists to resist Japan!' 'Save China!'..." His travel diary is referred to as 'The Classic Account of the Birth of Chinese Communism'. There is nothing poetic or even sociological so far in his book. Snow's claim to fame is that he was able to penetrate the Red Army 'blockaded' area because he had an invitation from Mme. Sun Yat-sen, (her late husband was the founder of the National People's Party). I am reading about Xi'an and, according to Snow, it was a pivotal city where Generalissimo Chiang Kai-Shek (Nationalists) was captured by his own military general by surprise and supposedly agreed to negotiate with the Red Army (Mao's side) to meet their demands and return to Nanking. This famous meeting took place right here, where I am. I continue reading to get a full picture of the turning of the tides that slowly eroded the Nationalists in this unique journalist account, written in the 1930's.

Snow begins his report from behind the walls in 'Peking', where he could hear Japanese gunfire. He claims the League of Nations (non-military commission as predecessor to the United Nations) had failed in 1931-33 to stop the Japanese invasion of Manchuria (Nanking) and thus lost favor amongst western intellectuals. Note: The League of Nations was the brainchild of Leonard Woolf (Virginia's husband), who had retreated to the countryside to support the war effort as a 'farmer'. The United Nations begins with military force against Korea at the 38th parallel, better known to Americans as the "Korean Conflict" after WWII; dividing it indefinitely as North Korea and South Korea.

I accidently came close to the N. Korean border on a trip from Japan following a tip by some German backpackers to visit an 'amazing mountain range'. I had ended up alone on a local bus without the German guys, stupidly traveling without my passport (left at the Japanese embassy for my student visa stamp in Seoul) and no local currency. One of the Germans had lost his passport and needed an extra day to go to his embassy before catching up with me. They encouraged me to wing it and not to worry. As they waved goodbye in the bus station, I settled in with no familiar faces. Most of the trip was pretty much normal with stops in towns along the way. Until we came to an unexpected military checkpoint. I kept my head down under a cap as the South Korean military boarded our bus with machine guns. I was the only foreigner in that group and luckily had made friends with my seat companion. He was calm and tapped me on the knee to assure me, all was going to be alright. There was no incident and we continued along as the sun was setting. I was trying to ask if he could help me change money when we arrived. Basically, he understood, but as it turned out we arrived too late, and all the banks were closed. I narrowly escaped the border check and ended up spending the night with my new friend and his buddies in a campground. They were a soccer team that also were rock climbers. Gallantly, they all squeezed into two tents and offered me a tent to myself. We sat around singing songs with the help of my harmonica (I always carry it). I was impressed with their friendliness and jovial companionship that could have been a disaster nearing the 38th parallel dividing free choice from freedom from choice.

Joan is still sleeping, and I am watching the sunrise with my novel in hand. I am beginning to understand the meaning of the 'Red Star' as the symbol of Mao's movement that I see here and there on people's blue (mao) caps. I bought a few pins as souvenirs yesterday, just in case they become extinct and later become a rare item for collectors. Joan did not want anything to do with them as she was afraid that she would have trouble at customs returning to the USA. I, on the other hand, did not intend to return right away in order to continue my global trip. Anyway, I am sending most of my Chinese treasures home in a package at the post office along with my blue mao suit. At times I prefer to blend into the blue crowd with my big straw hat and blue Chinese garb. There's not much difference from Jack Kerouac, a beat poet, showing up in Levi's to packed coffee houses reading poetry to mostly university students who wore suits. Since Kerouac was a merchant marine after losing his football scholarship in Princeton (with a knee injury), and considered a 'dropout', he entered the real world of workers. However, he never lost contact with his classmates, like Allen Ginsberg, prompting him to visit San Francisco and travel across the country, culminating in the writing of his famous book, "On the Road". Whereas Ginsberg was still wearing a suit when he recited his infamous poem 'Howl", and was reprimanded for the indecent language; he did not appear to be a 'worker'. Nevertheless, in *Howl* he did question all the drugs of the late 1950's that were destroying 'his generation'. (One of my father's high school friends overdosed, after failing in university, so I knew what Ginsberg was talking about). Today everybody is wearing blue jeans at university, women included. Of course, the bell bottom flare was not the classic 501 standard straight leg of the miners (origin of the jeans) that Kerouac dared to wear; he broke away from the norm that youth of the 1950's-early 60's wore in university. Don't forget, even the Beatles started out with short haircuts, suits and black ties.

October 5,1984

Joan's up and ready to get 'on the road'. Our plane ticket price had just doubled since Lhasa opened on September 1st, 1984. It was 322 Yuan round trip and now it is 644! Needless to say, we don't really care about the price hike. We board the plane with our hand luggage. Our larger bags have been checked in with bright orange tags, and safely put in the holding area. I am carrying my diary, books (feminist books from Beijing and Snow's book) and my camera in a shoulder bag, while Joan packed her bag full with snacks, our guidebook and the 'map'. The plane takes off and is shaking with noises that one could possibly interpret as 'falling apart'. I am hanging on for dear life in this rickety plane (seems left over from Russian Aeoroflop). I wonder if this was a good idea. How else were we going to get to Tibet? Thank goodness it was a short flight, only 1 hour and 45 minutes. After the initial panic, the plane levels out and I can see snow peaked mountains, maybe Nepal, and a very high peak; Everest?

We land better than expected on an airstrip that is a circular track in the middle of fields. I can feel a cool breeze gently cross my face and the sun is shining brighter than anywhere I've ever been. Is that because the air is absolutely flawless (probably void of any pollution in a 1000-mile radius)? I am indulging in the wide expanse of fields flanked by Tibetan mountains that surround us with this incandescent sunshine and pristine air. There is nothing here but a few farmers using the tarmac as a drying station for their grain. How did we end up here? It's a dream come true for a poet to scribble a few lines to remember this unique panoramic view with my senses ignited. No time to dawdle, Joan is frantically waving at me to hurry up. I just have to etch it in my brain. After all, our destination is Lhasa, her dream. Joan is walking faster to make sure we don't miss the bus. I reluctantly follow her and catch up; pulling myself away from this rare moment of serenity where time has stopped.

The baggage claim was invisible to us---we assumed the truck which was loaded up with baggage on the way to the airport in Chengdu would follow us to Lhasa. Sitting there in the bus with the Chinese waiting for 'something', finally the bus driver asks if we are ready. Everyone shouts in unison ">>>>>" ('ready' in Chinese, I suppose) and the bus begins to slowly move. Suddenly I notice orange baggage tags on the bags scattered around my feet. I panic, stand up and I turn to Joan shouting, "Oh no! Where are our bags?" The bus driver halts. A rough translation transpires, and the bus driver opens the door. I look on the tarmac; in a small fenced off area our two bags are a lonely pair waiting for us (baggage claim). While we were anxiously waiting for 'something', others were claiming their bags. Well, this is easier than pushing and shoving to find our bags! We hop over to rescue our bags like dumb foreigners. The whole group is laughing as we hoist our bags up and onto the bus. Joan is relieved! The bus driver closes the door and we are on 'the road' again!

I should clarify 'road' here. Since Lhasa just opened to travelers, the 'road' was actually being made as the driver (local bus) weaves around the workers chipping away at large stones to make gravel. Yes, that's right. I have never realized how gravel is made...from larger rocks! These women and men squat all day with a chisel out here breaking up rocks to lay down the 'new road' to Lhasa. I suppose there was only a path for walking before tourism? I have to admit, it is one of the most arduous rides of my life; a roller coaster over rocky terrain. No way are we going to give up! I grab Joan's arm. "Hang on. Tibet, here we come!" Joan laughs and points with her eyes to the rest of the bandwagon. We are the only ones looking out the window, while others just take naps, their bodies sway from side to side in a rocking motion, like being in a cradle with a lullaby. Wishing I had my bungee cord and rock-climbing harness to attach to the bus handrail, I don't let go of Joan or the seat in front of me.

Four hours later, give or take a bump or two, we arrive in Lhasa after numerous detours to avoid rock chippers. People are everywhere chiseling rocks and carrying rocks on their backs, both men and women! Back in the States we use dump trucks for this kind of work. Finally, my questions about the building of the Great Wall are answered; basic manual labor. Once we almost went over a cliff into the river; close call. I won't write to mom about this leg of the trip, she'll freak out. It is dangerous but later Joan says it is worth it. Glad she agrees! My head is beginning to hurt, but Joan is a trooper, reminding me that we can't tell our families everything. "We should just write about the exotic landscapes, people, and foods." Got it. We make a pact to keep these things to ourselves. She adds, "My husband will never let me out again on a trip." I reassure her, "Okay, I promise." The bus stops and doors fly open. People are shoving their way down the steps. We find out our ticket did not include transport to town. Luckily, two other travelers walked up and helped us to the main road---we had no choice but to drag on. Exhausted from the sudden altitude change from Chengdu at 1400 feet to Lhasa at 12,000 feet (more or less about half the height of Mount Everest---30,000 feet), we are pretty worn down at this point.

Surprise! Our authentic accommodation for individual travelers is a 3-story, newly constructed, colorfully painted Tibetan hotel, and the opening party is tomorrow night! Right now, I can't wait to get supper and then hit my bed. The Tibetans smile and point upstairs. I fully understand the meaning of 'lug-gage' as we trudge and lug our bags to the 3rd floor (dorm room). Joan introduces herself to a couple of roommates, Glen and Susie from Australia. My bag drops like a load of rocks from the road, and I vaguely hear the unexpected news; no showers or dining hall (kitchen incomplete). I pant, "What?" Glen kindly shows us from the window a dirt patio, where people are cooking on makeshift campfires. Joan clarifies, "You mean we have to cook ourselves?" Susie urges us to hurry up and buy a wok at the market and food supplies before it shuts down. Glen adds, "Don't forget the firewood. The best place to find some is in the alley." I turn around puzzled. "Where do we pick up firewood? In an alley?" Susie chimes in, "Yeah, you have to forage for anything that will burn." Joan looks at me in shock. It will be dark soon, so I tell her to hang out at the hotel and get a spot in the patio. I really do not want to lose Joan in Lhasa; I'd never be able to face her daughter (my friend Jill). I am 30 years younger and I take it upon myself to hunt for provisions. I am thinking we shouldn't tell this part to our families, either.

Outside in the market, I notice everyone is walking around in a circle in one direction. I do not dare to go the opposite way (bad karma). I follow the crowd around clockwise as the ritual prescribes. Finally, I find a market stall to buy a big black wok (cool, authentic Tibetan cookery) and utensils to stir fry for the next 7 days. We had decided to stay in Tibet for a week given that we probably would never be able to come back soon. I glance at the meat section, flies everywhere, fresh cuts, smells raw. I pass it up. I guess we are going to be Tibetan vegetarians. I see a lonely cabbage and carrots. I buy whatever seems edible which is not meat. My head is throbbing like someone is using it as a basketball to dribble down the court. I am all set, except I forgot firewood. Where the heck am I going to find that alley? I duck into the nearest one as the sun is setting fast. I miraculously stumble over a pile of splintering wood. I carefully take a few pieces under my arm and head back to the hotel. Where's the hotel? I ask in my broken Chinese. It's easy, since there are only 2 hotels. "Chinese? Tibetan?" I blurt out, "Tibetan". I meet Joan in the patio, and she smiles relieved. "Don't ask me how I did it. Let's just get this fire started." I pile the wood carefully so as not to get poked by a rusty nail or splinter and take out my handy lighter. Glad I packed this lighter at the last minute! Joan shines her flashlight on the cabbage and I use the wok like a cutting board and throw it all together. Joan gets some boiled water (always plenty of that around) from the hotel that issued us a thermos. We are about 10 campfires around the patio, all western backpackers. One guy has got a harmonica, another a guitar, and I have got that splitting headache reaching 'out of tune' proportions. The rest of dinner is a blur, and now I am in my bed under huge wool blankets. We survived our first day; mission accomplished!

Before I go to sleep, I ask Joan about showering. Joan tells me that according to the others, it's not necessary to shower every day because it's too cold here for bacteria to grow. She reports that travelers go to the public bath once a week and supposedly it's sparkling clean. She assures me that it will be a cultural experience because it's where all the Tibetan pilgrims bathe before visiting the Potala Palace. She's reading all about the tours for tomorrow. I am drifting off into never-never land with my never-ending headache.

October 6,1984

I wake up and my headache has turned into nausea, so I pass up the tour to the Potala. Joan found a couple of people to go along with, while I stay back at the hotel in bed. Glen says it's altitude sickness from the sudden ascent from Chengdu. Joan is fine and I am the only one with altitude sickness. I am prone to seasickness, but this is my first time at this altitude! Glen passes me some ginger to relieve my stomach and Susie tells me to drink plenty of liquids. It's a good to rest after girl scouting around for wood and veggies yesterday, the roller coaster bus ride, and the little sleep I got the night before last. I give up. My second day in Tibet is a no-brainer, bed rest.

I doze on and off all day. Joan arrives back excited from her tour and tells me I shouldn't miss it. She reports that the Potala is 'the most famous landmark' in Lhasa, dating back to the 17th century. It was the former residence the Tibetan Buddhist leader they call the 'Dalai Lama', and built in a mere 50 years! Glen remarks that it is supposedly one of the largest castles in the world. Interesting that he uses the term 'castle' because it looks like a fortress. Time for lunch, and I pass. Joan is invited to dine with Susie and Glen. I in my bed, snuggled up warm, and in a dreamy state. I wave at them, "Don't worry about me. I'm studying Tibetan painting and meditation". I'm on my back looking up at the colorful mandala designed ceiling. I am fine with my ginger tea. I guess I am doing a Tibetan fast today. Tomorrow I'll tackle the Potala.

October 7, 1984

Third day in Tibet, and my headache is gone! That's a relief! I am now ready to explore. Joan is joining a couple of Dutch women who are heading to the market. I am starving and gobble up the bread and tea provided by the hotel. As Joan is leaving, she points to the street where I can find a tour bus stop for the Potala. She gives me the time-table and I have about 5 minutes. We split up and decide to meet back for lunch. Surprise! I miss the bus, too late (I am still weary from air-sickness). So now what? I start walking, thinking maybe I can catch up at the front door to the Potala. On the way, I see a bunch of Tibetan women dressed in classic black Tibetan wool skirts (layers upon layers to keep warm) and they are heading in the direction of the Potala. I mingle in together with them. They smile and don't seem to mind. But when we arrive at the Potala, they don't go up the front steps to the main entrance. I separate from them and hike up the steps. I guess I was wrong. They are probably on their way to another temple. There is a sign on the huge door that states, "Closed for remodeling". I missed my chance yesterday with Joan! I turn back to check on the Tibetan women; they are waiting patiently at a side door. I'll follow them, why not? Maybe it's a special way to enter during construction.

At the small side door, they are waved in by the guard, and I hang out with them seemingly unnoticed. As soon as we enter there is a stone staircase leading downwards to darkness. A cold draft is whoosh-ing past me. I huddle in between the woolen skirts feeling protected as an innocent child swaying in a crowd; hanging on to mother's hem. They all light their candles, so we can see our way down the stairs. The aroma is a strange smell; it must be yak butter that Susie talked about at breakfast. The yaks are an oxen animal that is a universal plough work animal around here, providing milk and butter at the same time. I forgot my yak candle, but a nice young woman is handing me one before I can blink. Yak butter is a choking odor that I can only describe as a mix of dirty socks, leftover beans and musty old cooking oil forgotten in your grandmother's kitchen. We are descending lower and lower under the Potala. Where are we? A Chinese guy is pointing out statues and looks at me. He speaks a little English to explain. To him I am just another Buddhist pilgrim who came to pay my respects. He says, "These are the tombs of the Dalai Lamas of the past." I am thinking, you have to be joking!

I am looking around this cold and damp place that is more like a dungeon than a crypt. I did not read about this in the guidebook. Joan did not have this kind of tour at all! She talked about fancy rooms with wool rugs and scrolls. As we pass each tomb, the women chant a mantra in unison, and march to a slow beat. This is *way off* the beaten track. I feel like I am in an initiation ceremony in the darkest place in Tibet, but curiously enough there is a peaceful essence all around me. The women are kind and smile as I move along to the pulse of their prayers, as if I knew what I was doing. Maybe I had a past life here? From the underground yak butter dungeon, we ascend to the main hall of the Potala. I do not see any foreigners anywhere. The Chinese guy whispers, "There are no tours today, but since you came with the Tibetans, I'll let you come along." I nod gratefully, "She She". He smiles. I see workers on ladders arranging chandeliers to replace the candle lighting and obnoxious industrial floor lamps. Our yak candlelight tour is awesome! We stroll through the rooms like it was centuries ago. The women have stopped at a kind of throne, bowing. The Chinese guy waves for me to follow him and takes me alone around the halls. "They will be there for a while. You may be bored." I am stupefied. He apologizes: "Sorry you can't see everything today because it's officially closed." I let him know I am fine. I have seen enough for a lifetime! Let's face it, who gets to visit the tombs of the Dalai Lamas, unofficially? He whispers, "Please don't tell anyone you went downstairs." I shake my head. "I understand. I won't tell." Of course, I'll tell Joan, but she can keep a secret. She's going to flip out. I am kindly escorted out of the Potala and handed a pamphlet. I bow a bit, and I am on my way.

I stop for a moment to contemplate this massive 'residence' of a Buddhist leader. I wonder about the Tibetan teachings. This is far out of my league of understanding of Buddha and non-attachment. It must be a cultural thing. When I get back to the hotel, I'll ask Glen. He seems to know a lot about Tibet, far beyond our guidebook. Meanwhile, I read part of the pamphlet that says, "This structure is a homage to the people of Tibet who contributed with their labor to build this monument." Lee would say it's socialist propaganda. I say it's partly true, at least we can acknowledge the masons that spend their lives plastering castles, cathedrals, government buildings, etc. Why are we so fascinated by the architects? Without the skilled labor, a blueprint would be a faded archive. At least equal recognition could be a start. Moses did state the obvious back in Egypt. Slavery certainly comes in all colors and shapes. Is it possible devotees, (Tibetan monks) built it with glee or not? Anyway, I am thinking it's still ostentatious for a leader of monks. Shouldn't he be in some cave? Meditating for world peace? Glen told me the last Dalai Lama escaped overland during the 'liberation' under Chinese military force. Maybe if he had practiced martial arts like the Shaolin temple monks, Tibet wouldn't be Chinese territory. Nelson Mandela has been in jail for over 20 years to prove his point in South Africa to bring attention to apartheid; racial discrimination of white rule over native Black Africans. Cambodian Buddhist monks set themselves on fire to protest. I can't really say what's effective. Martin Luther King and Gandhi were martyrs for their causes. All leaders have their ways.

I look back over my shoulder at the sheer magnitude of the Potala and its presence in Lhasa. There is no doubt about it; it's not a simple Bodhi tree to meditate for enlightenment. Ever since spending time in Japan I have become tuned into Buddhism, and this trip was easier to start with a Buddhist philosophy; remembering the path is ahead whether there are clouds or mist, one must keep walking to find the Truth. It made me brave and not scared to fall into the dualistic phenomena based on success or failure. My trip will be a path forward. When I finish, I will find out the 'Truth' of my journey. I read Buddha quotes but never really want to join a group. I began to meditate on my own with a lotus pond outside my window in Japan. That was enough to contemplate my inner peace. But the martial arts practice does seem like a survival skill for anyone to defend their outer peace (especially a woman). I personally lean towards aikido and tai chi rather than karate. I never wanted to be a black belt and register myself as a weapon. Tibetan philosophy (some say) considers the negative side of a situation as a plan of action in waiting. This is not pessimism as much as a reality check. And a woman needs to be on guard, that's a fact.

I am heading back to the hotel to see if Joan has found anything interesting in the market. I am not looking forward to cooking, but tonight is the hotel's opening party and we need to eat early. Joan is on her bed, excited about lunch. "I found a noodle shop! We don't have to cook today!" I am totally in on that idea. No one is in the room, so I can tell her about my Potala experience. I am whispering just in case. Her eyes are popping out of her head in wonder! She remarks, "You even smell a little like yak butter. Fitting in quite nicely." I smell my blouse. "Really?" She laughs. "No, just kidding." She pulls on my sleeve and begs me to leave so we can eat Tibetan noodles and save ourselves the drudgery of being campfire girls. I'm not in the mood for wood gathering anyway. Besides, I am thinking it's not really nice to take all the wood. Tibet is pretty desolate as far as woods are concerned and I don't really know where the wood comes from. Nevertheless, all the buildings are made of wood with Tibetan flags blowing in the wind; it is believed that these flags are prayers silently being made by nature and humans together.

The noodle shop is no more than an open café with only one thing on the menu; a bowl of noodles (daily special). We grab chopsticks that are nicely displayed in a long bamboo container on the rickety table. We order the vegetarian bowl. Chopsticks in hand, we are waiting like two hungry kids. Everyone around us is Chinese and slurping away. We read that slurping means you are complimenting the chef with your enthusiasm. It's also a tactic to eat warm food and not burn your stomach! Here comes our noodles! These tasty noodles are what Marco Polo discovered on his travels to China on the silk route. I am just as happy to eat as not to cook. I ask for the bathroom and I am directed out back. As I pass the kitchen, I see a large pan of water on the ground with flies hoovering over the dirty bowls and chopsticks. When I get back to the table, I tell Joan what I saw. She reminds me, "Remember it's too cold here for bacteria. Don't worry." I grin and bear it. I want to believe her because I am too tired to fight back with an alternative; cooking on our own. Joan emphasizes, "This is the only restaurant in town. Just enjoy it. Remember while in Rome..." and I finish, "do as the Romans do."

Back at the hotel, we are told to rest up before the party. I gladly take a nap. No sooner than I doze off, we are being woken up to join the Tibetans downstairs. It's sunset and the westerners are ready to party. Joan warns me to be careful not to drink too much because of my altitude sickness and propensity to nausea. I am definitely not drinking! We change, wash our faces in the wash basin in the corner, and descend to the multicultural party. The Tibetans have decorated the dining hall (incomplete) with lights and color paper and have put out special foods to try. A western guy asks to put his cassette in the machine and a familiar song comes blaring out. This goes back and forth all night. Joan is holding on tight to me in this college party atmosphere, and I tell her to relax. The average age around the room is 25, but she hangs out anyway. She is not one to miss out on such a special moment! Next comes the special Tibetan beer mug, as big as a German beer mug. Tibetan women go around the room coaxing us to drink their home-made brew. They point at us to sip a little bit by pointing their finger on the glass. It's quite a tricky game to avoid them. To be polite, I take a small sip as a cheerful woman taps her finger on the glass indicating an imaginary line to finish. I feel like I am in a football game, getting to first yard for the other team (dreading a touchdown). She encourages me to do one more line; meaning to finish half the glass. I nod politely, and refuse. Joan doesn't even taste it. She gets away with not touching a glass due to her age. In that sense they respect her. The boys in the room are getting smashed! Joan and I retire early while Glen and Susie continue dancing. We are the sensible ones. I can't afford another day feeling bad and confined to my bed!

October 8,1984

Breakfast the next day is lonely, as most of the westerners are hung over in bed. Joan and I skittle downstairs and find leftovers from the party. We eat lavishly and smile at the Tibetan hostess. She giggles and remembers we did not drink much. She seems to be the manager in charge. She fills up our teacups and comments, "Good girls." We smile and Joan pulls out our guidebook. We are thinking about what to do next, but our money situation is running low. We need to change money. Here in Lhasa local money is better than Chinese official tourist money. Susie comes in looking a bit tired. I ask Susie on the sly, "Do you know where we can change money?" She gives me a hint to hang out on a corner near the meat market and ask a seller.

At the market Joan says she'll wander around (literally following the circular motion) innocently, while I'll take care of our money shortage. I tell her to meet me back at the temple entrance in 30 minutes. I go to the meat sellers and fiddle with my wallet; a young guy approaches me. He whispers, "Change your money?" I nod. He motions me to follow him quietly. We end up in his house where I change money. He introduces me to his wife and then they offer me tea. Why not? We are sitting on the floor cozy with these beautifully woven rugs, and it's a nice break from the cool air. As I bring the teacup to my lips for a warm drink, it tastes rancid! I squeal and he politely says, "Do you like it? It's yak butter tea." I can't refuse now, so I grin and sip. This is the price I have to pay for the good exchange rate. His wife offers to refill my glass. I nod, but she insists. Then the guy tells me about another offer: "How about a trip to another town? We can hide you and your friend under a canvas tarp in a truck." I thank him, but that's too risky. "Thank you, I need to talk it over with my friend. I'll get back to you." I look at my plastic mickey mouse watch (I didn't want to be too flashy---kid's watch) and realize Joan must be waiting for me. I politely escape with the yak butter taste lingering in my mouth. I stuff all the money in my pockets and head back to the market.

I wave to Joan, who is enjoying the whole market atmosphere. People are going round and round the market bowing in prayer formation on the ground until they reach the temple and enter through the right door and exit out the left door. It's a merry-go-round of prayers and Tibetans doing yoga postures (sun salutes). I tell her about the trip offered by the money changer. She mulls it over and finally declines: "I don't think that's a good idea." I can't even believe she was thinking about it! Hitchhiking in China, smuggled under a bunch of goods, on our way to Shangri-la! "Really, Joan, I definitely WANT to go." I wink at her, "Just kidding. I'm not crazy! After all, what would I tell your husband if we got caught?" She replies, "I'm not worried about him, it's my kids that would kill me." That's right, I would have to answer to my friend, Jill. I can imagine it now having to tell her children, "Well I lost your mother, while we were hiding under a tarp on our way somewhere in Tibet...". Joan changes the subject and asks me if we have enough money for the rest of the week. I tell her to reach inside my pocket. She pulls out some crumpled-up bank notes. Then she stuffs them back into my pocket, "Yuck! They smell like yak butter!" She's right, now my clothes really smell of Tibetan yaks. I joke, "At least I am trying to fit in with the Tibetans."

Tonight, I write to Dad about the enormous Potala wonder. He'll like this kind of news about the sheer enormity of it and its fortress walls---after all dad studied engineering. "Dear Dad, Guess where I've been today? You'll never believe it..."

October 9, 1984

After exploring the market again, we grab a bowl of noodles at our favorite noodle shop (only one in town). Joan tells me about a temple on the outskirts of Lhasa. I agree to go for curiosity's sake. Upon arriving, Joan looks up and down at these battered walls. Here we are dabbling in Tibetan Buddhism. In the wake of the ruins of this temple, we wander around faded wall paintings and crumbling pillars. I see a staircase and tread lightly, following it to the rooftop. Joan stays behind to check out more paintings around the ground floor. Suddenly, I find myself at a vantage point to look out over the countryside. The air is so crisp and clean here. The edges of the mountains are perfectly juxtaposed to the azure sky as if an artist had cut them out to fit against the backdrop. According to our guidebook, this building is mostly abandoned, with a small temple, and is part of a larger monastery that used to house 10,000 monks. I can faintly hear monks chanting in another part of the compound. I feel at peace here in the middle of nowhere, closer to the blue sky more than I have ever been in my life. I am content to blow in the breeze like a Tibetan flag. Joan is downstairs listening to an impromptu tour explaining the remains of paintings on the walls. I just wanted to feel the energy of this far-off territory that is a dreamland at this very moment in my life. I want to cherish the air, the clouds, the endless mountains that stretch out in every direction. I wonder where those Tibetan women pilgrims I met at the Potala came down from and how they survive the winters. The serenity is unbelievable, and I could come back here one day, just to hear these monks chanting, bells chiming and the wind gently passing over my cheeks. No wonder everyone has such rosy cheeks. The sun is bright, and the wind is endless. Neither one is offensive, but rather a blessing from the gods.

Joan and I trek back to the hotel to regroup with our friends for dinner. It's the noodle shop again. Where else are we going to eat? One guy is proposing a forbidden trip to a sky burial. Joan asks, "What exactly is that? Sounds fascinating." As he begins to explain what a sky burial is, I can hardly contain myself from throwing up dinner. "You see, the custom here when someone dies, their body is offered to the sky gods...vultures... he whispers. They crack the skull to attract the birds, and then you can watch from a cliff how the vultures dive in for the attack, picking apart the body. Eventually the whole body vanishes and the soul is liberated." Joan is scratching her head. "Why is it forbidden to watch?" I poke Joan. "Are you seriously thinking about going with him?" Joan is quite cold. "I don't know, it sounds amazing." I give her a definite answer: "Count me out! I do not want to be having nightmares for the rest of my life with that kind of 'cultural' experience." Everyone around the table is contemplating the idea. I slurp my noodles and ignore the chatter. I prefer to watch the flies in the washbasin out back. "Excuse me, nature calls. I'm going to the toilet." The flies are looking better day by day, innocently huddling over plates. I can handle this, but vultures picking out brains, no way!

October 10, 1984

Today is shower day. It's about time, since we haven't cleaned up properly in 6 days. Joan and I pack our toiletries and walk on down to the public bath. We are the only western women. Let's just say the only women not dressed in 800 layers of black skirts. As we wait in line, we watch women go in looking pretty gruff and ruddy from the dusty outskirts of Lhasa. Then they come out all spruced up, combing their wet, long, black hair. They are giggling at us with our pants and short hair. Actually, I don't feel that dirty since the air is quite arid and crisp. Nonetheless, a warm shower is refreshing. I suppose we could at least smell less yak buttery when we board the plane back to China. A week seems too short here. I was just getting used to this place, even though the food is kinda sparse. The Tibetans remind me of Native Americans in their faces, and even the silver-turquoise jewelry is exactly the same as that of the Arizona tribes. I remember studying in school that Asians walked across the Bering Strait and down to New Mexico and Arizona. I am witnessing it full scale and up close! It's definitely a small, small world after all.

October 11, 1984

Yesterday I saw the full moon rise. It was gigantic, coming up at the end of the main road like an outer-space ship! Of course, we are closer to the moon, up here at 12,000 feet! It was a magical moment that I will never forget. Today, I am packed, but not really ready to leave Lhasa. I could stay here for a bit longer. This is the only place we extended our stay more than four days. It was totally worth it! Joan got to see her dreamland and I got to smell like yak butter for a week. We opted out of the forbidden sky burial where we would have been smuggled over the mountains. Instead, we just enjoyed our last days in the market. I bought a few antiques, such as a worn-out tobacco pouch, incense burner, carved Tibetan wood beads, and a string of turquoise. Joan is still packing. She bought a lot of handicrafts and now is stuffing her bag. I urge her to hurry up or we'll miss our plane. We say goodbye to our friends in the dorm, the Tibetan hotel staff, and we head down the main road. We feel overloaded and did not remember how long the walk was to the airport bus stop. I ask Joan if she wants to hitch a ride. She is looking pretty tired and loaded down. Not one car is passing by. Suddenly I see a farmer driving a cart full of cabbage and flag him down. He nods and points to jump on. I throw the bags up and then pull Joan up. We leave Lhasa in the most comedic way possible. Joan smirks. "Hey don't tell anyone about this." I look straight ahead. "No worries, your secrets are safe with me." I don't know if it's the hitch-hiking or the cabbage that she is worried about. To me it was a lot better than dragging our butts to the bus stop and maybe missing our plane. We had to get back to Chengdu because we had heard about a massive market held once a week near a remote village called Dali. It was our only chance to visit a countryside town that was deep into the heart of China and just open to individual travelers like us. We had our permit and heading to the marvelous market would be amazing! Joan was all up for the trek to speed ahead to arrive on the exact day of the market. I could see it meant a lot to her, so I would make the extra effort to get us there on time. Little did I know it would mean traversing the back country of China, lost and hurled into precarious situations that only Joan could calmly deal with like an expert traveler (me tagging along for the ride).

We made it to the bus, dragged ourselves up the dusty steps, and sat down for the rough ride. The bus tires toppled over rock after rock down to the airport on the long and winding road. I am going to miss Lhasa and the Tibetans. The bus is full of Chinese and not one westerner---except us. Most of them are dressed in the blue and green mao suits, nothing to do with any Tibetan style woolen clothes that are as ancient as their religious ways. It's back to China we go. We arrive at the airport tossing and turning with a rocky road (ice cream) included. It's silly to call it an airport; no boarding gate, no baggage claim and one runway. Today they are drying some grain as usual on the tarmac. There are fields all around us and I see a family of farmers in the field next to the runway. I walk over and they are plowing the soil with their two yaks. The yoke is decorated with Tibetan color ribbons and have bells with woven colored collars. I don't know what to say to start a conversation, so I take out my Swiss army knife to entertain them. It's a real winner. Their faces light up as I show them this fascinating tool with all the gadgets. Mine is a simple one: corkscrew, nail file, knife, bottle opener, and can opener. The plane arrives and Joan waves for me to come back. I take a few photos and cherish this moment. The boys are wearing Mao caps and the women are wearing a combination of Tibetan skirts and Chinese jackets. The Tibetan rosy cheeks are a definite giveaway of their origins. I bid farewell and the man gives me back my knife. It's one of the few things I have from my homeland. I wave gently as the wind brushes my face like a Tibetan flag, saying a prayer in my heart. I am touched by these people and *their* homeland.

12

October 12, 1984

Here on the plane, we are trying to fasten our seat belts; mine is broken. Joan says, "Nothing's perfect." Really? It is like a daredevil motorcycle ride when you are all drunk at a party in L.A. Must have been the shots of tequila (worm included). We girls always felt we had some kind of control by delivering a sharp tug on the driver's t-shirt to slow down. Somehow that reckless stunt seems safer than this perilous act of zero control on a secondhand airplane in mainland China without a seatbelt. I am holding in my fear as we take off with engines sputtering, whereas Joan only has eyes for the Tibetan horizon. In two days, the big weekly market near Dali will take place and we can't miss it. Needless to say, we will be running after landing to catch a train in Chengdu to get there on time. The 7 days in Tibet have been memorable with the friendly rosy faces, whirling around the market in a subtle prayer circle, simple food and one ritual shower. Joan had told me, "When in Tibet, do as the Tibetans do." Tibet had been a far-out imaginary place to outsiders, where the magical 'snow leopard' supposedly roamed. That magical landscape still ignites one's heart. The dispute now in Tibet is whether their homeland has been 'liberated' from oppression by the Chinese or invaded; a sticky point. Albeit supposedly the Tibetan brand of Buddhism with non-violent dogma had brought a peaceful harmony to the region that suffered centuries of turbulent times. Nonetheless, a charismatic religious head, based in the humongous Potala castle with its brand of Buddhism spread throughout the northwest area of China, was not exactly in line with a marxist leader like Mao.

We saw the Chinese military presence around Lhasa, and they were mostly from the Han clan as I was told. Since the 1950's, Mao's Chinese authority has been patrolling Tibet, and the influence can be seen in minor details regardless of the flow of pilgrims from the surrounding mountains. Tibetan people had been in the midst of Mao's plan that was set on taking back so-called lost territories from their ancient past grandeur. According to Snow's book the Soviets had cut off financial support to Mao. Snow points out that Mao was left with guerilla tactics to survive, and his own form of communism based on patriotism rather than urban worker theories. Mao's agrarian stronghold was based in the western part of China stemming from his land redistribution campaigns. In order to directly oppose Japanese rule on Chinese territory, he proposed a 'Long March' on foot to confront the imperialists. Consequently, it became an inspiration for the 'People of China' to rebel at all costs, even though they were outnumbered and less equipped. In response, the infamous Nanking (northeastern China) barbaric massacres were carried out by Japanese forces, aimed at Mao followers who refused to give up. These atrocities remain etched in Chinese memories, as they witnessed the decimation of men, women, and even children by Japanese armies. Japanese people regret this part of their dark history that was designed as a fear mechanism for other Asians (invaded countries) to bow down to Japanese imperialism. I am still reading Snow's version of this political situation that also encompassed American and European presence during the entire fiasco. It's been a long and winding road for the people of China.

Right now, our plane has leveled out and there are no more strange sounds from the engines. I can relax and enjoy the last spectacular outlines of the mountain summits cutting the pristine sky. I am thinking about the hybrid dressing of Tibetan Lhasa women in long braids with Tibetan ribbons and mao suits, which contrasted dramatically to the Tibetan women pilgrims who came down from the outlying mountains in layers of hand-woven wool skirts with silver, turquoise earrings.

However, their unifying perfume of yak butter was distinctly Tibetan, as compared to us with only a bit of yak butter pocket money. Now it's a lingering memory that will stay with us until our 'people's money' runs out. We may need it in Dali. I do say the Tibetan yak aroma grows on you like mold on blue cheese from Paris.

The landing in Chengdu airport is rough, but no disasters. We race to get our bags from baggage claim, which is a proper enclosure with dusty bags everywhere, and the ritualistic pushing and shoving resembles digging for a treasure on an island surrounded by sharks. Well, it wakes me up from my stupor that comes from descending too quickly from Tibet and my slow meandering rhythm of walking around in circles for a week. We need a jolt to push us on to the next leg of the journey. Even though we have permits to go to Dali, we are on our own to find the right train once we get to the station. The taxi from the airport drops us off at the bottom of the metal stairs to the train platforms. I am fumbling with money, while Joan is trying to get the bags out of the trunk of the taxi. We don't have time to go to the post office to send anything home, so we'll just have to lug it all to Dali. Never mind that the bags are pretty hefty, Joan is as determined as I am to get to Dali for that market day. She hauls the bags singlehandedly in the direction of the stairs and waves me on to get the tickets. I run to the station information office at the top of the stairs. I am informed of the next train in the direction of Dali: 4:30. I easily buy two tickets with no delay (that's lucky!). Then I ask for the platform and a woman in uniform looks confused: "Meiyo". I turn to a man waiting on the nearest platform and show him my piece of paper with scribbled Chinese handwriting for "Dali".

I was smart enough to get the flight attendant on the plane to write it down before leaving the plane and repeat it to me. I learned it quickly and remembered: 'DA' like in LA Ti DA and 'LI' like Bruce Lee. A written note is essential because in China there are different dialects. We are headed to the countryside, so it's better just to show the Chinese ideogram, a universal language in China. I am shouting "DALI" and finally I am directed to the platform on the other side. I signal Joan and she starts carrying her bags up the stairs. I get mine and we are running to catch the train. The clock reads 4:15. We make it up and over to the right platform. No one is on the platform. That's weird. Maybe they will all rush in at the last minute. The train sign board above our heads says 4:30 but there is no train. The clock ticks 4:40. The uniformed woman comes up the stairs, and smiles. I ask, "The train? Where is it?" She taps her watch, 4:30 morning, not evening. Her English is broken but I realize military time means 24 hours; 4:30 means morning and 16:30 means evening (12+4=16). We have 12 hours to wait, but then we will miss the market if we stay overnight here! I see a train pulling into the station going in the same direction. I point to the train. She says, "Meiyo". I look at Joan. "Maybe we can go in the same direction and then change later." Joan agrees, and we hurriedly switch platforms (no easy task). The doors open, we jump on like hobos, and off we go! Relieved, we just hang out in the doorway, panting to catch our breath. Then, we calmly take a seat. Joan takes out some snacks and I am wishing we had gotten some lunch in Chengdu, which is a hub in the Szechuan province---my favorite food! Bummer.

No sooner than we sit down, the train stops, and everyone gets off. The train conductor comes to check our tickets, or so I think. Suddenly, two police officers are boarding the train and we are instructed to follow them to the police station. A nice attendant picks up our bags and we are escorted off the train. Joan looks at me dumbfounded, waiting for an explanation! I nod, "Don't worry, it's an innocent mix-up. I am sure they will help us to find a train to Dali." We are asked about our permits, once we are seated in the police station. We show them immediately and I pull out my Chinese piece of paper with "Dali" on it. A policewoman looks at our permits and nods her head in approval. She curtly responds, "Fine. You stay here and tomorrow Dali". No one really speaks English, but they are all very polite. I ask, "Where are we?" "Jianyang", comes the answer. Joan shrugs her shoulders. Then, another police officer enters adjusting his uniform that appears brand new, right out of the box, with distinct colors of gold and red. They all salute him, and we are escorted into his private office. Now it's getting intriguing. He is quite diplomatic, and he is accompanied by a woman helping out who speaks minimal English. He smiles. "You come from America?" We say in unison, "California". He looks at our bags, then our passports. Joan whispers, "Wait it out." Finally, he makes a call and waves us out. "You stay in hotel, and we give you translator." He rattles off something in Chinese, and we hear, "Enjoy lunch before room ready". I smile and say, "She Emiyo" and Joan follows suit, "She Emiyo". Now what? Joan tugs on my arm. "Play it by ear. Do you know pig latin?" Oh my God, I should have paid attention in grade school; it's the secret coded lingo that uses the last letter for the first letter. "Not really." Joan puts her arm around my shoulder like a mother and we proceed out of his office. She speaks the fastest English she can possibly spit out in order to throw them off guard. "Look straight ahead and don't take out your camera. Got it?" I just keep nodding my head and smiling.

We walk out of the train (police) station following the woman translator, and a black car is waiting for us. Our bags are put in the trunk and the translator goes with us, sitting in the front seat and directing the driver. We arrive at a hotel, nothing fancy and not at all vintage like in Shanghai or Beijing. The driver opens the door, and we carefully step out. Joan whispers, "Go with the flow." We are kindly greeted in the lobby by four smiling Chinese hotel staff. No registration, as the translator urges us to follow her. We are escorted through the lobby to a back room for lunch. The tables are all very large and round; arranged like a wedding banquet. There is a large, round, swivel tray in the middle of each table holding plates filled with all kinds of food---noodles, rice, glazed duck, crab, bamboo shoots, lotus root, dim sum. The room is full of grey mao suited attendees, and the décor is elegant. We are led to another room, where a beautiful Chinese screen gives us privacy from the other guests. We sit down and I notice the table is only set for two, with formal porcelain and pink cloth napkins. Three hotel staff are standing by our table waiting to serve us, I suppose. Without saying a word, dishes start appearing and are placed on the center piece tray for our pickings. Joan is astounded and whispers, "I never thought getting arrested would be so chic." I respond nervously, "Maybe they are fattening us up for the guillotine." Joan chuckles "Jesus, our last supper! Dig in, it looks scrumptious!" The waiters signal us politely to start eating. Joan turns the center piece and takes a helping of gorgeous crab and rainbow rice.

I peek out between the slates of the silk screen and notice there is not one person wearing blue or green. They are all (men and women) dressed in high collared formal grey mao suits. We are not crashing a wedding party, more like a government meeting! We definitely don't fit in but are treated as first-class guests. It seems like an oxymoron; backpackers arrested and then given a first-class meal. As we had heard about cameras being confiscated if you try to photograph behind the scenes, I don't dare pull out mine! Joan is more delighted than at any other mealtime in China. She must be starving for a balanced meal after having eaten Tibetan noodles for a week. My eyes are feasting on the cuisine that is absolutely mouthwatering and smells delicious! I try the soup first. As my tongue converges with the exotic aroma, I realize I have never truly tasted Chinese food. It is out of this world! Several dishes are delicately arranged in shapes and forms of flowers and figurines. It is as delightful to relish the visuals as it to savor the tastes. I thought the Szechuan cuisine on the train was tasty delicious, but that was just some spicy eggplant slapped on the plate. No comparison to being in the heart of the Szechuan province with the adornments of fresh flowers, greenery and stylistic arrangements! Even the tea is a world-class moment, with a fragrant Jasmine flower essence and rose petals floating in the cup! And to think I once thought the dining car in the trains or the leftovers from the tour were the pinnacle of gastronomy in Mainland China! How wrong was that conclusion?

Joan's eyes are moving faster than a pinball wizard as they keep bringing out more and more dishes to taste. I believe we are being served exactly the same meal as our government neighbors at the adjoining tables. Boy there is definitely a difference between the gray mao suits and the blue. Then again if we had known we'd be landing head first into a diplomatic luncheon of this caliber, we could have shopped around for a vintage grey power suit; at least to 'fit' in better. Are we still talking about a communist state of 'equality'? And the whole time Joan and I have managed to avoid the big white elephant in the room; the obvious difference of social classes. Lunch lasted a good couple of hours and now our translator pops in to take us to our rooms. Who knows where she was eating? She's wearing gray slacks and a plain white long-sleeved blouse. She doesn't quite fit in with the rest of the crowd, either.

We follow our translator upstairs in an elevator to the 10th floor and walk down a gorgeous, carpeted hallway. She opens the door, and we see our dusty bags sitting in the immaculate entry. I wonder if it is a marble floor. She lets us know that we can take a rest. We look around the room flabbergasted! It's a suite with two rooms; a king-size bed in each room and separate private bathrooms. There is a gorgeous soft sofa in the middle of the room and a glass table with a bowl of fresh fruit. I head to the bathroom and find the elegance of a first-class hotel. I pick up my backpack and dust it off to open it. Joan is laughing hysterically at my attempt to lean it up. Joan jokes, "You can take a girl out of the countryside, but you can't take the country out of the girl." I tell her to be careful opening her bag. "It may scare the translator with all those weird Tibetan souvenirs. Like that bone necklace that we don't know if it's yak bone or human left over from the sky burial." After investigating the room and a short rest, we are bored. Joan wants to explore the town. It's still early and we would like to walk off the lunch so we can sleep and get up early for Dali. We put on jackets and head for the door.

As soon as I open the door, the translator pops out of a room just down the hall from ours. That's strangely coincidental. She is rushing over to us. "Where are you going?" Joan innocently says, "We want to take a walk in the town." The woman locks our door, and then hers, ready to accompany us. I politely say, "That's fine. We can go on our own, we have been in China for over a month." The translator nods. "I go with you. You want to see the town square?" Joan nudges me. "Sure." We follow our translator who now is beginning to seem like our police escort. We suddenly realize we are not exactly free to roam around this town. I am wondering what the heck is in this town anyway. Joan looks at me sternly, putting her finger on her lips to shut me up just when I am about to ask a question. I glance at Joan and stick my tongue back into my mouth. No investigative reporting here, got it. We are led on our town tour with a tight leash, and I do not dare take out my camera which is tucked away in my shoulder bag under a towel.

There are bicycles and pedestrians on the streets, and everything looks normal. It's a grim gray industrial architecture, buildings in cement blocks, and functional. Except, when we get inside the town square, we see a group of people standing under an enormously tall pillar mesmerized by an oversized black and white TV screen. You will not believe what is playing tonight for entertainment. A Chinese soap opera? Nope. A martial arts drama? Wrong again. Joan grabs my arm and shakes me. It's a surprising black and white cartoon show: Mickey and Minnie Mouse! Now there's a vintage aspect of this town! Wildly funny to see a group of 'workers' in their blue mao suits smiling innocently at Minnie Mouse's squeaky voice. How could this be right? I can't even take photos of this historical moment! I tug on Joan's arm. "Can I just take one photo?" She almost freaks out and warns me not to even touch my bag. I have never seen Joan so serious. "Okay, don't worry. I'll just write about it in my travel diary". Joan knew that having already been to the police station, we needed to just get out of town quietly and be on our way to Dali. We circled the square once and the translator finished her tour. I point to my mickey mouse watch, "Time's up." Joan breaks a smile.

Back at the hotel, we are wondering about the plan to get to Dali. The translator (police) knocks at the door to present our hotel bill. I check it over and I see that the total is the equivalent of $100! I tell her that it is impossible for us to pay and quickly retrieve our bills from the past dorm rooms. I show her the receipts and demand that we pay less. She is looking at my hotel receipts and asks me to go downstairs to see the manager. I let Joan know that we are not going to pay that exorbitant price, especially since we haven't the money. I bring several receipts to prove we have not paid anything near that price on our whole trip in China. The translator shows the manager our receipts. He looks confused and then says something in Chinese. The translator tells me she will bring me a new bill, so we go back to our rooms. Knock Knock. A new bill is presented to us, and it is still too expensive. I insist on a lower price. She finally returns with a 3rd bill and it's within our price range. I accept and pay in official foreign money. I am saving our 'people's money' for Dali; besides, I can't explain my possession of black-market exchanges anyway. The translator says our bus leaves early, so we must be ready to leave at 5 a.m. for Dali. I ask, "Breakfast?" She tells us that breakfast boxes will be made so we can take them with us to eat on the bus. Lastly, she tells us, "Dinner in room tonight." We are so stuffed from lunch that we decline another meal. Joan points to the fruit bowl and pastries on the table. This so-called translator is bogus and obviously a police escort until we get out of town. I close the door and we have a good laugh about the bargain price of the room, $25. Joan is impressed with my bravo performance. We reckon that the hotel staff did not know how much to actually charge westerners!

October 13, 1984

We are up early, since we went to bed shortly after our (mickey mouse) tour. I was exhausted from the Tibetan-Chengdu-Jianyang trip and fell asleep without any thoughts. I wasn't going to second guess the police advice with our bus trip already arranged, even though today's schedule seems a bit weird and not anywhere in the guidebook. We are packed and ready to hit the road, and at 4:45 a.m. I open the door to go downstairs to wait in the lobby. No sooner do I open the door, and the translator is right on top of us. "Where you go?" I point to our bags. "We are ready to go to the bus to Dali". She is sharp, nothing gets by her. Joan picks up a couple of apples and closes the door. We carry our own bags down to the elevator, and once cramped inside, no one talks. In the lobby we are given our breakfast boxes. We walk outside and are led down the street a couple of blocks. There are a bunch of people lined up outside a local bus. Everyone is dressed in blue and green mao suits with lots of bundles. The bus is pretty rustic looking. I turn to Joan, "What do you think?" She turns to the translator. "How long to Dali?" A vague answer: "Three". Soon we are shuffled into the bus, and I poke my head out the window. "3 hours?" She nods her head. I take it as a "yes".

We are leaving this mysterious town and sitting amongst friendly faces, the vehicle resembles a hard seat train ride. Our companions are chuckling and pointing at us since we are the only foreigners. Joan is comfortable looking out the window and gently consoles me. "It's only 3 hours. Besides, it's kinda fun being on the 'off Latin beaten track'." She slept well and is in a jovial mood. I think if Joan is not worried, I guess we'll be alright. After all, she's a seasoned traveler, given her 30 years of wisdom way ahead of me. Her adventurous spirit is tame enough to analyze situations, yet not at all boring. She did admit that escaping the police harassment was a close call, so we should be careful. She wants to keep that part of our story a secret and just relay the exquisite meal with a first-class suite at 25 bucks! I am fine with that strategy, so I relax a bit and look at my mickey mouse watch to calculate our arrival. I am actually surprised this watch I bought in Hong Kong hasn't broken down yet. Joan thought it was silly to buy a cheap outdated watch. It's now looking like I am on the verge of a comeback; time warp trend setter. I don't think I'll ever part with it given its popularity is on the rise.

The bus is off the main highway now and we are cruising on a beautiful country road. It's absolutely picturesque, dotted with colors of fall and farmlands. It's 10:00 and the bus stops. I tap Joan on the shoulder. "It must be our stop. Look, it's more than 3 hours." Everyone is getting off the bus but leaving their bundles behind. A woman gestures to us, pointing to some small brick buildings; men are going around one side and women on the other. We figure it's a bathroom stop. We get off, thankful for the break. I've gotta piss, too! Joan and I enter the door with the "women" sign (I can read it). There are individual stalls, but once you get inside you are squatting on an open water canal (sewer) with everybody else's butt in the air. I suppose it's a 'people's toilet'. I can't hold my bladder anymore and Joan is already squatting. After I compose myself outside the bathroom, I quickly try to find out about Dali. No sooner do we step outside and there are two police officers adjusting their brand-new caps and waving to us. The whole bus load of people is waiting outside the bus. The bus driver is inside, closing the door. No one can board the bus. Great, now what? We walk over to the police, and everyone hovers around us, more curious than threatened by these supposed authorities. In fact, except for their caps, the police don't look any different from the passengers.

Joan is calm and takes my arm. "Come on, we know the drill. Just look innocent and show them our permits to Dali." The older police officer is holding some papers and then extends his arm so we can read it. He points to a line on the page. I realize it is a bilingual script to interrogate us, right there on the spot. We begin our roles; one by one the given lines printed on the page are recited. A series of questions begins, and it goes on and on. I see about 5 pages of script. It's getting late and we are not even in Dali. What's up? The bus driver gets off the bus to smoke. I turn to him and gesture for him to open the door so we can get on our way. By this point, the whole group agrees with us. The bus driver takes a long drag on his cigarette. I insist by waving my permit to Dali, and he turns to the police officer. They scan the script for one more question. Joan answers quickly and walks to the bus driver. Now elders are a different story in China, and her motherly appearance softens the bus driver. He puts out his cigarette and opens the door. The police give up their charades and we confidently step up to retake our seats. Boy, this mother-daughter act is quite useful. I am sure if we were two young backpackers with our cameras clicking away, it would not be so easy to escape. The bus engine sputters and we are back on track. The passengers are amused and smiling at us again.

I turn to Joan and alert her that we may be lost. It's been way over "3 hours". Joan digs in her bag and takes out the National Geographic giant poster map of China. We attempt to pinpoint our location on the map by asking the people around us. They look confused and we realize the whole map is in Roman letters, not Chinese ideograms. Joan and I are baffled. I pull out my small piece of paper with Dali written on it. Then the people understand. Thank goodness! They say in unison, "Ming Tian". I search for my dictionary, and I decipher the word. I point to the word and Joan gasps, "Tomorrow?" In Chinese, tomorrow means bright/sky and I hear a chime from behind me, "Ming Tian". The woman in front of me is gesturing to sleep and then repeats, "Ming Tian". I am thinking about that "three" that the translator said. I reluctantly relay my thought: "I think she meant 13 hours or 30 hours." Joan replies, "Or even 3 days, not 3 hours!" We both agree that we can't stay overnight in the next town, or we'll miss the market! Joan calmly looks out the window. "I get it, we have to just wait and see. It's such a nice day, let's just enjoy the ride for now. I think we have 5 hours to go." She's probably right. This ride is a rare opportunity to see the 'real China', and it seems like we have been adopted by this group.

It's around 12 noon, lunchtime. I'm getting hungry and our breakfast boxes are long eaten up. There is a crowd up ahead on the road and the bus is slowing down. It's market day today in this village and there are loads of activities. The people are dressed in colorful outfits that do not resemble anything we have seen in Mainland China, Hong Kong or Taiwan. The women wear their hair in braids interwoven with colorful ribbons wrapped around their heads. Their dresses are long blue layered tunics, and they are wearing special shoes. We must be getting closer to Dali because they seem to be the Bai people that are a minority group of southern China, as described in the guidebook. This is precisely why we are visiting Dali and the big market day; it's supposed to be a spectacle insider view of the minorities and their handicrafts. The minorities in China do not adhere to the mao suit attire, so we see few in this crowd. Joan signals a woman passing by to see what she is selling. She has a beautiful basket with goodies inside. Our seat companions are reaching out the window to buy something from her. It smells delicious and fresh. We watch how much they pay, then Joan, sticking her neck out, gestures to the woman. She buys 2 pieces. We are starved so anything will suffice. I bite into the bread slowly in case it's fatty pork. Yummy! It's a cheese bread with onion flavor. I poke Joan. "Quick, buy a couple more, before the bus takes off moving faster." This is not an official stop and we are just passing though villages. It's Sunday and all along this part of the journey we have been watching colorfully dressed people go to markets. I wish I could take out my camera, but we don't want another chance meeting with pseudo police.

Our bus companions share a few more goodies with us before we start to move along at a faster speed. I must have nodded off because the sun is getting lower in the sky. I look at my watch. Now it's 4:00 p.m. Finally, we seem to be arriving to our destination. The woman in front of me turns around and says, "Dali, Ming Tian" and folds her hands against her ear to tell us time to sleep. As we enter the town (end of the bus line), I notice people hitchhiking, even women alone, on the side of the road. Big trucks are mostly passing them by, but some trucks stop to pick up passengers. I look at Joan and point them out. "Joan, we can hitch the rest of the way. Dali has to be really close. We've been traveling for nearly 12 hours! Joans checks her watch. "Well, it's not dark yet and I figure we have about 2 more hours of daylight." The bus pulls into the covered station and I whisper to Joan, "Let's sneak out the back and follow the road to the place where the women are hitchhiking. Okay?" Joan nods. "Yeah, okay." I remind her, "If we don't keep moving, we may be picked up by police and have to stay an extra day in this forsaken place".

The bus stops in its parking spot. Then there is the usual confusion with pushing and vying for packages, bags, chickens, bundled up infants and everything else one can imagine on a local country bus. People are scrambling to unload their wares and grab their child. Meanwhile, we avoid the bus driver's eye and disappear behind the other buses with our luggage. Heading out of the station without looking back, we find ourselves next to a woman who is hitchhiking. I have my handy piece of paper with "Dali" written on it ready to show a driver. I really wish we had mailed some extra things in Lhasa or Chengdu, because the extra bags bought in Hohhot are a pain to manage; at least they are holding up, rain or shine. They look flimsy but actually are quite sturdy. It helps to fit into the local landscape since just about everyone has at least one of these bags mixed in with their luggage. The woman gets picked up after about 3 trucks. Now it's our turn. The trucks are analogous to army trucks back home; green, monster wheels, except the driver with a green or blue mao jacket. A truck filled with massive, oversized logs whizzes along; passing us up. The driver was all alone and could have easily fit us into his cab. I suppose he doesn't want to deal with foreigners. An empty truck zooms ahead and doesn't even stop to look at us. Finally, a truck pulls over and the driver gets out. We show him our destination, "Dali", and he smiles. Then he hoists our pathetic load of baggage on top of the cab and we climb up the two steps to sit beside him in the cab. Joan takes the window as usual, and I am next to the driver and the gear shift. I repeat, "Dali", and he smiles again, nodding, which I interpret as "Yes I am going your way." Joan chimes in, "She She". I try to ask how long, but no success. We'll just have to wing it.

Our driver is in his late 30s and reminds me of a family man working his long day on the road. His jacket hung on a nail behind the seat and nothing else personal is visible in the cab except his cigarettes. After about 2 hours, it's definitely sundown. Joan is taking a nap and I have my eyes peeled on the road. Suddenly he stops at a house with a lot of other trucks parked outside. Don't panic, I am thinking. I tap Joan on the shoulder. "Wake up." The driver gets out and signals us to come along with him. Oh no! Police again? Joan says, "I don't think it's a police station, look at all these trucks. It looks like a truck stop." I hope she's right. We shyly follow our driver into the house, which is actually a place to eat. He tells a woman at the counter something and we follow him to a back room. The people are all smiling and acting friendly to our driver, who seems to be a regular customer. We sit down and a country dinner is served to all of us. I really wonder where Dali is. Joan is not even thinking about Dali, just slurping up the noodles. "Come on, eat up, we don't know when our next meal will be." I follow her lead and as long as it's cooked, I am not worried about my stomach. I am still surprised we have never gotten even a tinge of loose bowel movements on the whole trip. We finish off with tea and dessert. I'm feeling as stuffed as a steamed dumpling! Our driver insisted on paying, so we let him and don't make a big deal about it.

Less than an hour later on the road, the driver stops and walks around to the passenger's side of the truck with a giant flashlight. He shines it on the left side of a building; we see the Chinese writing on the wall. I translate, "It means woman". Joan blurts out, "Oh I get it, it's a truck stop bathroom. Great, I gotta go after all that tea!" I can't agree more! The driver waits by the truck, hands us his flashlight, and starts smoking a cigarette, looking out to the road. He's a real gentleman. We hop back into the truck cab after the pit stop. It's getting darker and darker down the road. There are fewer and fewer vehicles on this stretch, and we seem to be going up a mountain. Joan is fast asleep on the window seat, and I am glued to the road. I am starting to freak out because every time a truck comes in the opposite direction both trucks turn off their lights! There are only two options: high beams or no lights. Of course, high beams would blind the drivers, so they politely turn off their lights. It's a crazy game and I am so nervous. Now I am slapping the leg of the driver every time he turns off his lights as we swiftly go blind for a few seconds. He is smiling and totally calm. Am I the only one worried here? Joan is sound asleep content, (probably dreaming of Dali), the driver is smiling without a worry, and I am in total panic! We slow down and pass the logging truck that did not pick us up. It is now parked on the side of the road and broken down (more like broken through). The logs busted the cab driver's window. He must have stopped short. Logs went right through the passenger's side. Shit! That could have been us with a log through our heads. Our driver pauses to check and is waved on by the other driver. What the hell have we gotten ourselves into now?

There is no turning back and I have to just trust the stars for our safe journey to frigging 'Dali'. This leg of the trip goes on for 6 more hours! The driver pulls up to a hotel and we just make it before they close at midnight! The driver gets out first and signals me to stay in the truck. I am numb from the 'formula one' blind race! I shake my head, no objections by me. My nerves are shot, and my body feels like it just went through a war zone. While the driver is inside, I notice he left his jacket. I slip some people's money into the pocket, knowing he won't accept it later. I poke Joan. "Hey sleepy head, we're here." Joan surfaces from her slumber, "Really, I was having such a nice dream." I quip back, "Good for you. You missed all the fun." Joan shuffles in her seat. "Where are we?" Exhausted, I snap, "Dali. Where else would we be?" Joan perks up. "Great! We made it! Good job." The driver comes out of the hotel, and someone opens the gates so he can drive in to drop us off at the door. Our luggage is piled into the lobby, and I kindly shake the driver's hand. "She she". He chuckles and waves us on to go in. Reception smiles and asks, "Ni Hou?" How am I? I can't even put English words to describe my state, let alone Chinese...

13

October 14, 1984

The next morning, I wake up late and Joan is nowhere to be seen. I get dressed quickly and go downstairs to look for her. As I am approaching the reception desk, I hear Joan say, "We are *not* in Dali?" Joan is looking down on a piece of paper as the receptionist explains. I want to die! Where are we now? I rush to the desk, "What's going on?" Joan turns to me, "Don't worry, we are just 20 minutes away." My heartbeat slows down. "Alright. Let's get a taxi." Joan whispers, "Hey smarty pants, we are in the countryside, no taxis. They are offering a cart to take us." That eases my mind. I'm not so worried anymore, since we are so close. "Fine, let's get breakfast and then trot over to Dali." Joan winks at the receptionist and pulls me away. "I gave him some money to muster up a clean cart." That's a good idea, I nod in agreement. Who knows what condition a 'cart' could be in around these parts. "Good thinking! I'm starved." Joan gently hands me a bag. "Don't get your hopes up. This is not a tourist hotel." We go back to our room and pick through the breakfast bag; 4 Chinese dumplings and a tea bag. Glad I ate all my dinner back at the truck stop last night. Joan reminds me when we get to Dali the guidebook says there are country restaurants with plenty of food. "Well, at least we are not in hot water anymore with the police and got a kind receptionist to arrange our transport; beats hitchhiking". Right, I am looking forward to the market, but actually anything slow and easy after that treacherous truck ride last night is fine by me. I still have jitters from that ride. I let Joan know that she missed the best part of the trip with our driver and the nerve-racking headlight games. She only replies, "Really? I had a great sleep! Thanks for keeping an eye out for both of us." She winks at me, kindly.

We walk downstairs to the lobby and the receptionist is pointing to the door, "Your transportation is ready". We drag our bags outside to the promised cart complete with a farmer and his horse. Joan inspects the cart like a den mother for the boy scouts. She turns my way and signals me with a thumbs up. It's clean except for a few straggling pieces of straw. The farmer quickly grabs our bags, and like bales of hay throws them onto the cart. Then he invites us to sit up front with him. Joan whispers, "First class service to Dali." I shake my head and we wave goodbye to the hotel staff. We arrive easily on a country road lined with trees, and it's a wonderful way to enter the mystic town that has eluded us for the past 24 hours.

Dali is set on the picturesque banks of an immense lake flanked by mountains. According to our guidebook it is the capital of the Bai people, who once enjoyed a considerable influence over the region. Dali is in the Yunnan province where 'over half of the 55 listed national minorities' in China claim their homeland. Here in Dali, a combination of indigenous folk culture and Buddhism once flourished, supporting festivals and over 200 temples until the cultural revolution swept through the area. The nearby mountain temples were 'razed' to the ground followed by a devastation that 'suppressed' the Bai people; a similar scarring outcome to most of the minorities and Buddhists throughout China according to our guidebook.

Our cart driver knows exactly where to go, and we are escorted to the lobby of the foreigner hotel. We get our dorm room and it's full of backpacks everywhere. However, not a single westerner is in sight. Joan says, "They must have left already for the big market." The place is empty except for the staff. When we ask the hotel staff about the special market, no one knows what we are talking about. How are we going to find that market? We were told that it was outside Dali, nearby. We walk outside and see a western guy in the courtyard. "Hey, do you know how to get to the market?" He replies, "Which market? Dali market? Easy, just go out and turn left." Joan quickly chimes in, "No, the other big market outside Dali? The big special weekly one?" The guy shakes his head. "Oh, you missed the bus. It left early this morning and takes an hour. Anyway, the market ends around 11." I stammer, "We can get a cart!" Joan checks her watch. "I think it's too late. It's already 10." The helpful guy remarks, "She's right, no way you'll make it." I sit down defeated. Joan tries to cheer me up, "Come on, let's go explore a bit of Dali and get some food". We thank the westerner and head out to eat. "Really, Joan. We missed the market?" Joan consoles me as we sit down at one of the recommended restaurants on our list. "Let's face it, we saw marvelous markets yesterday on the way during the bus ride. I'm sure it was totally better than that special market backpackers rave about." I perk up. "I guess you're right. That was pretty exceptional, and the cheese bread was such a surprise!" Joan, gives me a little motherly support, "Thatta girl! Cheer up".

We stroll around Dali after eating and go window shopping. I stop at a shop with fake teeth. That's a novelty we haven't seen before. Back at the hotel, we end up in the dorm room for a rest before our next move. I take a nap on my bed and soon I am woken up by backpackers rustling around. Joan asks them if they've just come back from 'the market'. "Yeah, it was great, but the bus left too soon", says a German guy. One woman adds, "I wish we could have continued into the more remote villages." Joan winks at me. "Why?" Her partner replies, "It would be chancy, but imagine what the 'real' China is like." Joan grabs me and takes me out of the dorm room before I can speak. She whispers, "Don't talk about our secret expedition from Chengdu to Dali. Let's just keep that between us. See, we were really lucky! No one had that experience." I add, "Yeah, I guess you're right. It was so far off the map, who knows where we were." Joan, continues, "Better to keep some things quiet and not draw attention to us." I concur, "Deal. Let's just act dumb and find out more about Dali." We go back in the room, and someone tells us about a bike rental shop. I am totally up for that idea to bike around the lake. Joan passes and prefers to just hang around town walking to look for antiques.

October 15, 1984

I'm standing in front of the 'Happy Bike Rental' holding my handy tourist map (especially made for clients). On one side it has the main spots of the town drawn out like a Monopoly game board in English and Chinese. I appreciate the bilingual version in case I get lost. Let's see, there is a handicraft shop, bank, Catholic church (really?), hospital, women's and children's health center, cinema, People's government, single pagoda, police station (staying away from there), two bathhouses and a horse race field, amongst other things. On the back of the map are the outlying areas around the lake with warnings: 1) Please don't climb the mountain, for it is dangerous (also in Chinese), 2) Please don't go sightseeing in a boat, for it isn't safe. If you want to go, please go to Xiaguan and take a ship. On the mountain side, there are markings for the Serpent's Bones pagoda, the Big Stone temple, Zhonghe Monastery. In the lake there are 3 islands: Jinshu (Gold Comb) Island, Chiwen (Red Writing) Island and Yuji (Jade-like) Island. In the center of the map, it states: "There are 19 peaks in Cangshan Mountain. Between the peaks there are 18 clean streams. People always say 'Silver Mountain, Jade Lake'. Most of the population here is Bai nationality. The culture of Bai is one part of chinese ancient culture." Interesting that 'Bai' is capitalized and the word 'chinese' is not. Just above that is another statement: "Dali is famous for its 'four views'. They are Xiaguan's wind, Shangguan's flowers, Cangshan's snow and Erhai's moon. Erhai Lake means that the lake looks like an ear in Chinese; 'Er' means ear, 'Hai' means sea". There is also a 'Butterfly Spring'. Well, that's a lot to digest. I turn it over again to get my bearings here in town. I see the "Happy Bike Rental" clearly marked on the map as my starting point and an easy route to Erhai Lake just down the road to the right. It seems I just need to follow the road out of town. Actually, I notice all the roads to the right lead to the lake and all the roads to the left lead to the mountain. It's like an I Ching board game - mountain or lake? I choose lake. Off I go!

Nice to be out of town on a country road and feel the breeze. I see the lake coming up and the mountains are also in plain sight. In the distance I spot a waterfall. That looks enticing. I start to head out that way beyond the lake. It's October and the rice is being harvested. I stop for a glimpse at the ritual of thrashing the golden rice stalks laden with grain in a giant basket. People are smiling at me, and I gesture with my camera to take some photos. They pause and pose for me. I get up close and they hand me a bundle of stalks to thrash along with them, side by side. I'm not a pro, but I remember it in Japan. I partake happily and it's a once in a lifetime experience to hang out in the middle of this rice field with women and men who seem to be well-fed folks. No one looks hunger stricken. In fact, along the way during the whole serpentine Dali route I never saw any beggars or hungry looking people. You have to admit we were *way off* track from the tourist places and in the 'real' China, so you can't just make that stuff up. If we hadn't gotten lost on the way to Dali, I would have thought the Chinese government gives you permits to control access to unwanted images of starvation. Now I am rethinking the whole permit thing, as China is just not ready for tourists, even backpackers. Right here, though, I am enjoying the freedom to bike around the lake and a chance to explore a waterfall.

I wave goodbye to my rice buddies and hop back on the bike. This sturdy mode of transport feels safe and just my speed. There are few trucks on the road and more bicycles than walkers. Suddenly I come across a group of people standing around a truck. What happened? As I get closer, I realize they are actually butchering a cow! Right there on the side of the road. Talk about 'road kill'! I slow down and stop. Not because I am a bloodthirsty tourist, but I eye a gorgeous authentic Dali basket under a woman's arm sitting in the truck. I couldn't care less about the bloody scene taking place. I avert my eyes from the main event (fresh rib eye steak) and gesture to the woman with the basket. I take out some of my yak, smelly people's money (I knew it would come in handy from Tibet) and offer it up for the basket. Now they are all snickering at me. I approach the woman and the others convince her to bargain with me. At first, she thinks I want to buy the vegetables in the basket. She begins to hold up each one to see which one I want to buy. I signal "none". Then I tap my finger on the basket. They get a real charge out of that idea! She empties the basket and hands it over as I hold out the money. It's a deal. I don't even take out my camera, since the blood is now heavily flowing in the street. Reminds me to always ask for 'well done' meat or fried chicken! I hop back on my bike and continue to the waterfall.

As I get closer to the waterfall that now appears quite far from the lake, I begin to wonder about the rain clouds high up on the mountain ridge. I am not sure I can make it back to town before the clouds burst. I forgot my rain poncho, too! What's the point of packing a compass, a flashlight and a raincoat if you forget it on a lonely mountain path in the middle of China? Idiot!!! I look up at the inviting waterfall one more time, but I'm not exactly sure I should risk it alone. I look the other way and cherish the view; rice fields and the lake below. It's pristine here, and quite the Buddha land. I absorb the essence in my memory and click a few photos. Then I am off to get back to Dali. I take another route along the lake and enjoy its serenity. Looking up to the mountains, I don't have to imagine what's on the other side. We've already been there! Sometimes imagination should be enough to quench the thirst of a traveler. I will have to take note of this idea for next time. Just enjoy the view, stupid! Forget about 'greener pastures' on the other side.

Luckily, I get back just in time before a light drizzle. 'Happy Bikes' is 'happy' to see me. I was gone for longer than expected, so I pay for the extra hours. I suppose losing a bicycle is pretty sad, but worse is probably losing a tourist! Who knows the penalty? I meet back up with Joan at the hotel, who is giddy with her exuberant report of Dali. Then she notices my basket and bursts out, "What's that?" I casually say, "Oh this? I found this on the side of the road in a group of people. And you?" Joan jabbers more about her morning and a bathhouse that has massages. I am really not hearing this right? "What are you saying? You want to take me to a massage parlor?" It gets worse. Joan continues, "There is this blind guy and herbal medicine treatments." I reply, "Joan, are you out of your mind?" Joan insists, "Just come with me. Everyone has told me it's such a treat. Aren't you tired and sore after that truck and bus ride? Not to mention all those 'hard seat' train rides." She's right, I am exhausted and sore from all of it! Joan shows me on the identical map that I got from Happy Bikes. She's got a tourist map, too. She suggests stopping by today before lunch and booking one for tomorrow. A hot bath sounds pretty nice given that we share an outside toilet in the hotel. It's a little hike behind the woman raising chickens... if you need to wash after the toilet, she'll invite you for a spout of cold fresh water. Nothing to write home about.

October 16, 1984

The bathhouse is around the corner where there are marble tubs cleaned with a red antiseptic liquid and a mop. We watch as the ritual is performed. The bath is 60 Yuan, and a massage is 80 Yuan. My masseur is deaf and mute, but we communicate just fine, since I am now an expert in sign language by this point of the trip. Joan gets the blind man. I do not care really if my guy is blind, or whatever. I just put my head down with a sheet over my back and he begins. It is superb and I am starting to believe massage was invented by the Bai people! It was just what I needed. At the end of the session, I am handed a cup of pleasant medicinal tea from his daughter made from herbs according to the diagnosis from the masseur. I tip him and the woman laughs. I tell her (she speaks English) it was the best massage in my life! She actually had to wake me up. We find out it's a family run bathhouse and we go back the next day; I request the same guy. I tell the woman it's my last visit, and I am going to miss all of it. When I am finished and dressed, my masseur hands me a small black and white picture of himself in a mao suit. His daughter translates for him and she says that he does not want me to forget him. I put his picture in my worn-out leather passport pouch that I carry around my neck for safekeeping and I assure her I won't forget him. It's a lovely souvenir from Dali along with the basket.

Our favorite restaurant in Dali is the "Garden Restaurant" because it really is a garden café. It serves hash browns and eggs in the morning and the menu is in English. At the doorway, a sleepy dog is content with leftovers and never bothers us as we enter. An old, sweet woman welcomes us with a twinkle in her eye. The patio is full of potted plants all around with birds singing as we eat our meals. At our first lunch, we ordered fried tomato with cheese for an appetizer and then waited a long time for the main dish---fried chicken. As I went to the bathroom, I spied the old woman plucking a chicken clean with her versatile hands. That surely was a fresh meal! We also tried the "Lunch-room" where we exchange money for cigarettes (always carry a couple of packs to trade for emergency supplies-hint from the guidebook). The Lunchroom staff speaks nicely to us and offers a great veggie plate as an alternative hippie happy meal. Dali is a world of wonders. One morning we noticed marijuana weeds about 15 feet tall hanging over a garden wall at the end of the main road! Backpackers are garnering a few buds every day and smoking in the hotel courtyard. No one even cares. Joan is a bit uppity about it, but she's getting used to it. The weed is being dried out on the balcony. One guy is smoking from a bamboo bong he found in the market made for tobacco. Joan whispers to me, "Be sure to check your bags for seeds or loose leaves before we leave. I want to depart from Dali, not be deported." I try to humor her and snicker in a low voice, "It's not like we went to the golden triangle (famous area between China, Thailand and Laos) and got opium stashed in our pockets". Come on lighten up." Joan doesn't want us taking any risky chances, pointing out our recent happy-go-lucky police 'close encounters'. She adds, "We are officially 'aliens' on this soil and it would be nice to remain friendly". Get my gist?" I concede, "I get it". I nod like a scolded child sent to the corner with a dunce cap plopped on my head.

All in all, Dali has been a real treat from the rest of China, with its small villages scattered throughout the rice fields, horse carts jingling down the paved shady streets on the outskirts and smiles of the Bai people. I will never forget Dali. We book our tickets for the 11-hour bus trip to Kunming. I am curious to see the terrain in bright sunlight! I wonder what we missed on that wild goose chase, taking the 'off the beaten track' truck route at sundown. Who does that? A couple of nutty, independent women from L.A.

14

October 18, 1984

We are on our way to Kunming today and there are quite a few westerners at the bus stop. Our bags are overfilled, and we are ready to send things home at the post office in Kunming. Joan is a bit sad leaving Dali and I don't blame her. I've got my Dali basket under my arm and I am wearing a big farmer's hat that I bought at the last minute. It will come in handy to blend in more easily in crowds with my blue mao suit. Joan thinks it's a bit over the top but agrees it's good for blocking the sun from my face. I love it and will always cherish it! We had a great time in Dali (once we got here). It was relatively easy going with a good mix of getting to know the locals while hanging out with other backpackers and comparing notes for the next part of our trip. A lot of us had the same guidebook (the only one available) and the latest news from the grapevine. Dali was not even mentioned in the 'Off the Beaten Track' book. We had found out along the way. That is the state of moving around in Mainland China as an individual traveler; things are changing week by week. Regions are on the move to open and get permission from the central government to issue permits, and hotels for individual travelers are beginning to pop up to accommodate us. Our bags are safely put away and Joan grabs me to get a window seat. She just wants to relax and enjoy the scenery we missed on the way up to Dali in the dark. Here we go, the bus starts up and we are on our way back to an urban area. The first part of the trip is smooth, but then the bus starts to climb up the mountains. I am looking over

Joan's shoulder out the window. It's a nice sunny day and clear with a bird's eye view. The road is on the edge of a cliff! I am thinking it's a good thing I did not see this coming to Dali. Now, the bus is moving swiftly around curves going down the mountains.

Memories of my trip in Taiwan traversing the Taroko Gorge on the East-West highway are coming back to me. Back then, the first day on the bus was filled with magnificent views of marble rock faces along the gorge that took my breath away in awe! We stopped half-way to stay at a temple in the middle of the pristine mountains; the fog was drifting in and out of ravines adding to the poetic atmosphere. During our short overnight stay with the monks, I contemplated the universe in cosmic harmony. In the morning, I made a donation to help rebuild the roof, and my name was painted on a roof tile in remembrance. I reluctantly pulled myself away from the temple to continue the journey across the gorge, with some cliffs falling off 10,000 feet. I boarded the bus and unfortunately was thrown into a nightmare with a rally bus driver racing to the finish line. At one bathroom stop, I refused to get back on the bus and waited for the next one. My intention was to visit one of the wonders of the world and I would do it again in a flash, which is what I saw (my life in a flash) as I caught a glimpse of the edge of a sheer rock face! The second bus driver was quick, but less daring. Nonetheless, my name remains painted in a temple somewhere over the clouds deep inside a mountain range on the island. Taiwan was a seesaw of amazing and terrifying moments! I almost got hepatitis, slipped when climbing a famous mountain at sunrise, and almost got killed on that bus trip! Yet, the serene blues, greys, and white palette of the marble gorge and temple experience was like stepping into a time-less ink painting of a Chinese master. Luckily my traveling companion was studying Chinese and could negotiate our trip through the trials and tribulations.

Now I am reminded of how the bus drivers here in Asia seem oblivious to danger on mountain roads. I am sure we westerners are just too pampered. Joan pokes me and comments, "Look how beautiful the valley is!" I need to be more like Joan and just enjoy the ride. I casually respond, "Yeah, you're right. It's gorgeous, breathtaking!" The eleventh hour has arrived, and we are pulling into the Kunming bus station. This is a large city and no comparison to the last few places we have visited. We are now in the hub of the Yunnan province just north of Vietnam where a railroad was built connecting it to Hanoi. At one time this area was a bustling stream of foreigners and trade. We get settled into our hotel after a short reasonable wait and sleep to our hearts content the first night.

October 19, 1984

We begin the first morning slowly reading about what to do in Kunming. Teahouses are an interesting aspect of Chinese culture featuring musicians, storytellers, and opera singers. According to our guidebook, Kunming is one of the last places left to enjoy them. Marco Polo even found this city remarkable. There are handicraft stores devoted to wares from Yunnan's minority peoples, which we do not want to miss. We needed an extension on our permits, too. Just before we were leaving for Tibet, we were told in Xi'an by rude officials: "NO, never!" I am dreading the fight for a bonified extension.

The Kunming government office is a breeze for obtaining our extension. The woman official comes in casually apologizing for her lateness: "Good morning, what do you need?" We get the extension effortlessly and that eases our minds. I can already feel the cosmopolitan sensibility here with the polite treatment from the officials. With our extension, we can take it easy for the rest of our trip. It means we do not have to rush out of China by plane. We can also leisurely enjoy a riverboat ride through the ancient mountain gorges near Guilin that is featured in all tourist pamphlets promoting China. We want to spend our last few days just being lazy travelers. Next, we are off to the handicraft store for our last souvenirs. Kunming has three stores that specialize in minority people's handicrafts from all over Yunnan. Joan is delighted to browse all three stores. I agree to go along with her to only one shop and then we split up to explore the rest of the city on our own. Kunming is easy to navigate even with old narrow streets that remind me of the French quarter in Shanghai. Joan feels comfortable exploring on her own so we agree to meet up for lunch going our separate ways.

I stroll around the streets with my farmer's hat and end up in a store that sells musical instruments. I fall in love with a Chinese sort of violin—an 'erhu'. I have no idea how to play it and ask for a few tips. The woman selling it tells me there is a teahouse where musicians hang out in the evening if I want to learn how to play it. She writes down the address and name in Chinese. Perfect! How hard could it be? This instrument only has two strings. She sells me a set of spare strings to take home. It's a lovely treasure with the hand-carved, wooden tuning knobs and fresh snakeskin wrapped taut around the sound box. I can't wait to show Joan!

Back at the hotel, I am waiting for Joan to go to lunch. Then she appears as if she just came back from shopping in Chinatown (San Franscisco) with her overflowing bags. She sits down and without missing a beat, starts chattering about the town, while showing me her newly purchased handicrafts. I slowly open my new erhu case and take out my musical treasure. Her eyes light up! She runs her fingers across the fresh scales of the snakeskin. Taunting me she whispers, "Did you find out what kind of snake that is?" Cooly, I respond, "I did. It's python". She jerks her hand away. She blurts out, "Are you kidding?" "No, and I got extra strings in case they break." Joan jokes, "Did you take a course in snake charming in case you need a skin replacement?" "Ha, ha, ha. I'll cross that bridge when I come to it. Isn't gorgeous?" Joan smiles and pats me on the back. "Yes, it is and quite impressive"! She adds, "and original."

I give her the plan for the evening: "Tonight we have to go to a teahouse so I can learn how to play it." She thinks it's a wonderful idea. I emphasize that the recommended teahouse is not even in the guidebook. I comment, "We can hang out with the local musicians!" Joan interrupts me, "Oh, speaking of locals, I almost forgot to tell you. I wandered on a back street and met three old women drinking tea in a living room." Joan continues, "The door was open and I poked my head inside. That's when they invited me to sit down. I gestured to them that I had to go, pointing to my watch. I signaled I would be back later with you." I am floored, "You did all that talking with sign language? Very impressive." Joan wants me to go back with her on the way to lunch. "You'll love it! It's the real deal and these women are older than both of us, so they don't seem to care about spies telling on them." That's fine by me. Women get braver as they get older, I guess.

Joan has a good sense of direction and easily finds the house with the elderly women. They are still there sitting there on a couch sipping tea. Joan signals from the door, putting her arm affectionately around my shoulder. They wave at us to come in. I don't really know what they are saying, but one is pointing at Joan's wedding ring. Joan is nodding and the time goes by as slow as ancient tea ceremony but not so serious; all of us giggling about almost nothing. Nonetheless, it is a nice break from the streets and shopping. We are just women chatting (sign language, more like it) on a sunny afternoon like geese; floating on a calm river after a long flight. Nothing special, but actually a very delightful and friendly encounter. Joan gestures pointing to her watch that it is our time to go. They all smile in unison and I ask for a photo. They nod in agreement, and I capture their genuine, grinning faces that reveal a secret language amongst sisters; without even looking at the camera. Surely, they thought we were mother and daughter. We wave goodbye for the last time. Outside, we stroll in silence for a bit before reaching the restaurant. We both know we will never see them again, but it was worth the moment---frozen in time, admiring the lace doilies on the table and floating gracefully through an unspoken conversation that only women's intuition understands.

Evening is approaching with sundown and Joan wants to find the teahouse before dark. We have an early dinner and then stroll along with our scribbled piece of paper in Chinese to find the musician teahouse. We finally find the traditional teahouse, confirmed by a young guy on his bicycle hanging out outside: he checks out the name on the paper and points inside. There is an indoor tearoom and a porch where the musicians are playing. I walk up the steps to the porch with my music case and they smile. They make room for Joan and I on a wooden bench (familiar hard seat) to sit and join them. I take out my brand-new erhu and signal to find out how to play it. I hand it over to one guy and he tunes it for me. Then he hands it back to me. Well, I reckon I can give it a try. Did I mention I have years of hammering on piano keys embedded on my fingertips, lungs fit for blowing the wind in and out of a bamboo flute and even agile lips to whistle across a C major harmonica at a campfire jam session in South Korea? However, nothing could prepare me for the enigma of this simple two-string instrument. Where to begin? Besides, Chinese music is not western music. To our ear it sounds like a crane falling from a branch, struggling in mid-air. So even though I know how to play classical piano, I am thrown off by the unfamiliar scales and tones. This instrument is made to accompany an opera singer with a high-pitched voice. I pay attention and learn the basic way to hold it and move the bow. Each musician is showing me a technique with their own mastery as if it's as easy as pie. In my attempt to wield the bow between the two strings, a horrible sound squeaks out. Laughter spreads out in every corner. Joan is hysterical and is bursting at the seams. After several attempts, I decide to forego my lessons until I get home. I put it back into the case and we order tea. Lovely pastries come with the tea, and now I can appreciate the music even more than ever. I hold up my recorder while they play a lovely song. Then I play it back for them. It seems like it is the first time they heard their own music! Sincere smiles all around as we step down into the street and wave goodbye. Music is lingering on the fences as we round the corner back to the hotel. I proudly carry my erhu safely in its case like a new friend.

October 21, 1984

Today we wake up happy in Kunming after a couple of days of roaming around tasting foods in the cafes and laughing at the cages parked outside with animals and fish tanks for fresh delicacies. We are reminiscing about our teatime on a lazy afternoon with sweet, elderly women and the unforgettable jam session one evening with local musicians. We have some free time before lunch so we split up again to make use of our time wisely and agree to report back to the hotel later. Alone I walk a bit without an agenda, heading in no particular direction until I hear some commotion up the street. I get closer to see what's going on. I turn the corner and there is a team of people with ropes trying to tackle a huge task; taking down a giant Mao statue! The guidebook indicated that Kunming had nine Mao statues in the city placed in prominent places. People in this city are dressed in mixed outfits, some with mao suits and others in cotton long sleeves and slacks. I hang out a while watching this crucial event, but don't dare take out my camera. I am glad I have my farmer's hat on and nonchalantly approach the crowd. I am a witness to a turning point in Chinese history. It's a blip on the radar screen of 5,000 years of history, but still a moment to remember. Mao is tumbling down in history.

After that historical moment, my eye catches a shop window full of masks. I nip in and can't pass up the paper mache pigs, monkeys, clowns; all made for Chinese theater. In a corner in the back of the store, I discover hand sewn caps decorated with long colorful tassels protruding from the top and hanging over sides. My mom will get a hoot out of these gems; she's loves to dress up! There is so much variety here in Kunming for the arts. It's starting to drizzle, so I decide to take a bus back to the hotel. As I am looking for the bus stop, this Chinese guy in a sports coat (how weird) asks me, "Where are you from?" I was going to take the bus, but decide to walk and chat for a while, pulling out my rain poncho. He walks with me along the street and tells me he is an English teacher. It's a rare occasion to speak English he confides. I answer his basic questions and our conversation is light and easy. He doesn't seem nervous to speak to a foreigner and leisurely strolls along with me. I suddenly see a boxed ad behind glass (not the news-paper) depicting a living room with one child dancing around in the middle of his parents. I hesitate and ask him to wait. I want a closer look. He comes up to the glass of the ad display beside me and flatly says, "Abortion advertisement". I am stunned and he repeats, "Abortion ad". We walk further together, and I probe him a little about family planning. He tells me I could visit the Health Department to get more information on the one-child policy (abortion ad). I take the opportunity to ask him about the Mao statue I just saw being toppled, so to speak. He says, "They are being taken down because it is not good to worship someone." He lets me know where the Health Department is on my map, but comments that it is closed now in the afternoon. We come to another bus stop and I am ready to go. If I want to go to the Health Department, he agrees to meet me at 10 am at the bus stop tomorrow morning to help me find the building. "Oh, that's very kind of you. See you tomorrow, then. Thanks again."

October 22, 1984

Today, Joan couldn't care less about the Health Department and leaves me on my own. The English teacher doesn't show up even after 45 minutes. I guess I am really on my own to hunt down the Health Department. I discover a building that looks official and venture inside. There is a leprosy exhibit in the lobby, which astonishes me (another reason to keep foreigners segregated in safe areas). I slowly scan the photos and then inquire about my destination. A woman writes it down in Chinese in my notebook to help me. After a few people direct me here and there, I find the right building but the front doors are closed. It's one of my last full days in Kunming so I take a chance and yell to a woman I can see walking around inside. I ask about the family planning department. She signals me from the window to go around back. Two police guards are at the back door and can't speak English to help me. So, I just walk in the door and the woman comes to take me to a special department for 'family planning'. It is closed. She calls another woman but they both get frustrated with me. They call out to a guy down the hall. He writes a note in English. We communicate back and forth with notes and he keeps saying it is closed. He finally gets fed up and writes, "Come with me." He comes out from his office and takes me through the back streets of Kunming.

I have no idea where I'm going, but I stay close behind him not missing a beat. We are walking in the rain and finally we arrive at some foreign department (I can recognize the Chinese word for foreigner, nothing more). After arguing with the guard, I am allowed in. A government official dressed in a leather jacket and turtleneck sweater (70's style) greets me---he's a tourist liaison. Then, he invites me into his office and I am able to interview him. He begins: "Good afternoon. I understand you would like some information about family planning." He tells me all about family planning and its benefits to the people. If everyone (100%) in a factory abides by the one-child policy, the whole factory is rewarded. I am thinking peer pressure, but only nod my head to indicate I understand. Besides, couples are given an extra monthly payment if they remain with only one child. I record the whole interview and take notes. He doesn't seem to mind. Our discussion is loose and our subject content drifts at times. He speaks freely on a variety of subjects. I ask him about rations and people's money. He explains that the extra subsidies are a grade system by doing certain things projected by the government. For example, "Intellectuals get an extra subsidy of about 15 Yuan a month." I'm thinking, the whole system is based on money? I keep nodding. I comment about the train prices. He replies, "Yes, there is a big difference in prices between hard seat, hard sleeper and soft sleeper. But the people don't travel very long in hard seats---short distances." I beg to differ, but I don't mention my own experience. I ask, "Which do you usually ride in?" He nonchalantly responds, "Oh, I go by plane." I was so shocked! I stopped writing for a moment and tried not to look surprised. "And is that subsidized by the State?" He answers with no hesitation, "Yes". I ask him to write down his name and address in my notebook. "I'll send you a postcard from California." He proudly writes his name, Wu Zhongning, in English and Chinese. After the interview, I understand how people are able to buy clothes that are not mao suits and other amenities that are not the standard government ration.

October 23, 1984

Kunming is interesting from many angles, and I could explore it for days. Nonetheless, we need to go to the post office before leaving for Guilin. I want to travel light and Kunming is a reliable place to post our souvenirs. Joan leads the way since she already studied the map, when I was been busy packing. I carefully wrapped up my Tibetan and Dali treasures, not to mention my prized musical instrument. I really hate to part with it, but I can't see myself hanging out on the road tweaking it and deafening my fellow backpackers. We finish sending post cards, packages, and airmail letters back home. I am sure my family will love the stamps and have fun looking at the novelties I gathered. Leaving the post office, I notice some of the plants outside along the wall which are labeled with botanical names in English. However, there is a huge marijuana plant in the middle of them, like a companion plant to offset the smaller plants in the group. There is no label on it. I take out my camera to get a picture of this novelty. I am reminiscing about Dali and giggle at this decorative addition on official grounds. I ask Joan to take a picture of me in front of it. "Hey, who is going to believe me if I don't get a picture?" She is reluctant but finally agrees. She quips back, "Alright, but keep me out of the picture. I don't want any trouble at home."

We go back to the hotel and grab our bags because we have a train to catch. We don't want to miss our precious train that is a combo ticket with a sleeper. It's 36 hours to Guilin, and a hard seat all the way would kill us! We want to enjoy this final leg of the trip and arrive semi-rested. Of course, that is the plan, but who knows what will happen!

15

We have been in China about 7 weeks (almost 2 months) and reluctantly coming to the end of our *Ripley Believe or Not* trip. It has given two naive, dreamy travelers (Joan and I) an inside view of 'communist' China and a bit of expertise in these parts for surviving. Something I can add to my resume for job hunting *or not.* I can understand why Emilio let go of his guidebook so easily; and is not too keen on doing any more trips to China for a while. I cannot even imagine taking on Italians to deal with all these obstacles; knowing my own family disputes that arise at the dinner table just to pass the olive oil or get grandma to sit down with us to eat! I am grateful though for the tips he wrote in the margins and basic advice he told me how to cope with the idiosyncrasies of Mainland China---don't give up to get a bed. I am looking forward to sharing stories with him, if I ever get to Italy on this globe-trotting adventure. I'll write to him when we get on the train; I've got plenty of time to pass between sundown and sunrise.

We are departing from Kunming and heading to Guilin on one of our last train rides. We have been lucky to secure a hard sleeper for the evening. I am glad Joan and I came with our thrifty spending habits, as it gave us a taste of how it feels to live here under a variety of conditions. Actually, I am glad I got to know people on a one-to-one basis regardless of our nationalities. I bought a painting from a woman this morning who was quickly showing me her art in a makeshift illegal open market under a bridge. Yunnan province is famous for its artists and I rolled it up as a treasure---a watercolor painting of pomegranates on a tree branch. It is nothing fancy, but her smile and hands told me a story I never could have found in any art gallery in the world.

The first part of our train trip is slow as usual and fine with me. It gives me a rare moment to let my mind meander along the landscape without worry, knowing Guilin is a popular destination on the *beaten track*. Nothing special on this train ride, but we are comfortable with our hard seat companions. I glance across the aisle and see a man smoking tabaco in a water pipe. I nudge Joan and she cracks a smile. I casually take out my camera and get a snapshot of this hilarious scene. I turn back to Joan, but I hold back my giggles. I realize today she is extra quiet, staring out the window in a dreamscape.

Evening approaches with the last slivers of the sunset glow over the rice fields as we are escorted to our hard sleeper. Sadly, we leave our hard seat companions behind, but we are butt raw from the day trip. Here in the sleeper, we are sitting on the lower bunk bed with our Chinese roommates across from us. Night comes quickly, cheap dinner boxes arrive (saving money) and then an attendant comes to make up the beds. Lights out and silhouettes of the rice fields flash by like a movie. In the middle of night, a couple of authorities peek in the door to check on us. The Chinese train officials don't bother me anymore like they did on our first trip back in September. At first, I was scared of their presence checking all the tickets with an authoritative stance. Now after weeks of hanging out in trains, I am used to them and greet them with a smile. After all, we are 'tourists'---guests. I fall asleep to the rocking of the train like a baby in a cradle. The shifting of the rails is melodic and when we wake up, we will be closer to the famous Guilin.

October 24, 1984

Morning starts with an announcement over the loudspeaker at 6 a.m. I lie there wondering if I'm the only one sleeping. I am on the top bunk of 3, I look down on my companions. There is a woman still sleeping and Joan is still asleep. The speakers continue and I imagine it's the tai chi exercise lesson for the day. Who's going to do tai chi on the train? It probably also includes some government radio news, too. The morning sun is nice and it's a rare moment to enjoy waking up on a train. The day goes by slowly back on our hard seats. At one of the village train stops, Joan hands out balloons to a couple of kids from the window. Soon kids from the whole village are running to Joan's window. A man next to us yells at the kids to say "Thank you" in English. I try to get a picture before the train takes off. Joan is laughing and loving it! These little friendship trinkets need to be given away, no use in taking them home. Smiles move in waves like boomerangs; from one face to another and back without a word.

Guilin is probably the most well-known landscape that depicts China as a land of enchantment, with the Li River peacefully winding through a maze of limestone cliffs, alluring tourists to its destination. National Geographic (with its origins from Washington D.C.) naturally were here to promote China after US diplomatic relations reopened; dedicating a 30-page spread in 1979. Of course, their story is a somewhat officially recognized rendition of how China operates behind the scenes that was unknown to American visitors since 1949. I find my experience neither better nor worse than that journalistic report, but it's uniquely mine. Here in Guilin, I am relaxed after our overwhelmingly complicated trip across the continent that never could have been predicted. We arrive late and don't have any trouble getting accommodations. Joan suggests we take it easy for a couple of days.

October 26, 1984

We sign up for the riverboat tour, and as a poet, I am delighted to hear the poetic fairytales that accompany our magical ride as described in our guidebook. The cultural value of the artist-poets that dates back millenniums in China, created a finely tuned language of pictograms to communicate concepts beyond syllables. Moreover, these philosophers attempted to explain the cosmos and nature as merged into one seamless scenic backdrop for humans to appreciate with storylines and illustrations. We amble along the road at the end of the town. We are not in any hurry. It is one of our last days to enjoy being so-called tourists. On the way to the docks, I stop at an official tourist shop to buy a black ink painting of these landscapes for my mom. It will be a nice souvenir because she is a painter, too.

As we float down the river, our guide softly points out the highlights from ancient folklore. One set of limestone rocks is a flower bouquet and each rock formation is a bud waiting to bloom. Another set of mountains is a dragon that had stopped here at the Li River because it is so beautiful. Another mountain is a bird who had landed for a drink of water and drank so much it couldn't fly away. We look at the cliff formations and try to follow the storylines.

I am thinking about who had enough idle time to do art and write stories. China must have been poorer in years gone by... or maybe there was a great class difference, and some had free time to write and paint. We visited a mountain retreat yesterday that was so remotely hidden in the cliffs that it could have been one of their poetic resting places to contemplate the cosmos and nature overlooking the valley. The sign posted to sell tickets was funny: "Buy your ticket comrade." It was such a mishmash of cultures in China. There is the overladen communist BLUE motif in the hard seat section of the train, government officials living the high life in GREY, cultural monuments of ancient lineage (what's left after the Cultural Revolution's sweeping devastation) and younger people eager to understand western lifestyles; learning English to read and chat with foreigners.

Right now, I am sunk down on a small wooden seat in a slow boat in China, navigated by a woman steering with the tiller in one hand and holding a baby on her knee. I am immersed in this exquisite afternoon light that spills over into the emerald, green silken waterways. I suppose other tourists begin their dream trip here as an introduction to China, while we are coming out of a dream backwards. Our painstaking effort to see the 'real' China was a dream and has been fulfilled. I guess that's what makes humans a unique species, with each mind on its own path. Joan looks peaceful peering up at the limestone cliffs that stimulate the imagination. I have a nice painting in my bag that captures the Chinese essence of this place. Nonetheless, I am thinking about my own mom. She loves to paint and draw, especially nature and portraits. Gazing at this woman at the tiller, I can imagine my mother sitting in this boat with me; I can almost hear her pencil on the pad as she sketches the Chinese woman with the scenic cliffs in the background.

When my father was working late, she would put us to bed and paint her large oil canvas to pass the time alone. We never saw her actually paint; it was her secret hidden life as a midnight artist. As kids we just knew the painting was changing slowly like an elf came every night to dab a few strokes of paint, transforming the canvas overnight. No one ever talked about it, either. It was just the 'spare room' meaning I had to share a room with my sister so my mother could have her studio, per se (along with the encyclopedias, sewing machine and the filing cabinet). She decorated our house with motifs of famous artists such as Degas, Rodin, Monet. It just never dawned on me how much she loved the classics and the importance of visual aesthetics. We grew up surrounded by beauty with a theme for every room. The living room was early American country. The dining room was tastefully dotted with impressionist paintings of Paris. The stairway was framed by Degas ballet dancers beside a magnificent full length *Blue Boy* on the landing. We first saw this original painting in the Huntington Library collection---a hideaway excursion Mom gave us to round out our cultural life. I suppose the La Brea tar pits (a school field trip) was too obtuse to be considered artistic. The kitchen was cutely decorated with Dutch blue plates and wallpaper to match. Rodin's sculpture, 'The Thinker' was on top of the filing cabinet contemplating life. Her passion was art on a daily basis, but it was also her own private world of creativity in the twilight hours.

{I was fortunate later in life to experience my mother's delicate brushstrokes on canvas firsthand. I found a soft spot during the most challenging time of her life due to her lack of hearing and onset of dementia. It inspired me to

seek alternative ways of communicating. I prompted her to take out her paints from the garage and teach me some of her techniques. I was in the middle of a doctorate that required painting and any help was welcome. At first, I was disappointed that we could not carry on complicated intellectual discussions as usual. However, as we painted together, the secret life of Jeanette (Mom) was revealed for the first time, namely to me. I feel privileged to have been side by side with her as she dabbed her brush across the canvas or to have watched her rhythm as she spread black charcoal on the white paper with a final touch of an eraser with her deft hand to round off the edges of a still life pear.}

Joan coughs and wakes me from my daydream. We step out of the boat on the Li River drenched in a peculiar serenity that reminds me of the grasslands. Back to reality, at the hotel I am finishing Snow's book, which has a strange ending when he returns in 1942-43. He was working for the *Saturday Evening Post,* and ran into a Chinese intellectual, who commented on the situation that led to dire straits for the Chinese people. They were suffering under the Japanese barbaric modes of quelling the Mao rebellion, while foreign western governments stood in the wings thinking they could 'defeat Japan through China'. Snow listened to the Chinese man: 'After all you saved the Kuomintang (Japanese backed government). It's your baby now and you cannot avoid responsibility for its actions.' Joan and I definitely have an expanded view of 'communist' China from our wild and crazy adventures.

I really liked that feeling of traveling by boat today on the Li River, so I suggest we don't take a train back to Hong Kong. We find an alternative: a hydroplane down the Pearl River. We make plans to head to the town where it leaves from every day. Although it's fast and modern (an unexpected mode of transport in these parts), it's a perfect scenic ending to our trip. The breeze of the boat feels fresh. My eyes are teary as I know this trip will never happen twice; it has been a once in a lifetime journey that I will cherish forever!

16

Epilogue

March 1985, Bangkok

I am sitting on my bed waiting for a call from the US Embassy; hopefully someone will turn in my passport. I was so distracted at the post office calling home for a last-ditch request. I am out of money and broke again, but do not want to give up my dream to travel around the world! I displaced my wallet and passport at the telephone counter after the depressing news; "Sorry NO! Come home if you can't afford it".

I open a cheerful letter from Joan addressed to me 'Post Restante' Bangkok. It helps brighten up this dark, damp room. She writes about the latest news back home in the swing of 'life' as mother and wife. Although, she confesses that she is planning another trip and that keeps her motivated to carry on in the midst of daily chores. I am happy for her!

Last time we saw each other was the end of November (1984) in Hong Kong. We had spent a month in Nepal with stopovers in Bangkok. When she left, I was a little depressed and out of sorts. I didn't quite feel fully recovered after the massive shits I got from Nepal (spent the whole flight in the bathroom). I let my guard down in Kathmandu and didn't use my own mug or silverware because everything seemed so 'clean'. There were bistros and cafes everywhere and

I thought I could relax. Wrong! I could not even stop the diarrhea with the drugstore remedy. Good thing I hadn't gotten sick in the mountains at the base camp in Annapurna at 12,000 feet! Finally, after I could hold something in my stomach, I told Joan I would be alright. She had to get home anyway, considering she was already a month late! Her husband was not so happy she had missed Thanksgiving and was worried she might follow me on my world trip.

Well, I'm back in Bangkok, but no Joan. I am here in Apple Guest House and 'Mama' cooks the same menu every night---fried chicken in pork fat with white rice. You pay for your room and food at the end of your stay. I order the greasy plate every night, which is starting to show up as pimples on my face. I never had problems like this! Meanwhile, I wave at the backpackers who constantly invite me to join them for dinner to roam around the streets eating the incredible noodles, ginger chicken, etc. I politely decline. I have my outfit for teaching English, and tomorrow again I will beat the streets in search of a job. As I walk around, I only see Sanskrit letters on the signs above the buildings. I have faith; something will show up positive, or not?

I start my letter to Joan with just the good news. I briefly explain how I followed some French travelers to a tropical island in Southern Thailand for two months with only coconut trees, sandy beaches and snakes. I celebrated Christmas and New Year's in Singapore with Aussie divers (fresh off the boat from Antarctica), before that I hooked up with Americans at Chung King Mansion and ended up on a boat trip to Singapore! I survived it; crossing the South China Sea in a 33 ft. sailboat dodging pirates and crew mishaps. I denied my panic-stricken memories from that jaunt across one of the seven seas by overindulging these past few months to calm down. Hence, my dire financial situation. I couldn't tell my family that's the reason I needed money. I didn't tell Joan either. I did let her know I would write a book about that great adventure on the high seas, because it was so exciting! I know she will believe me given our history in China! I can't think about it right now, though. I put down the letter and start contemplating my situation here in Bangkok.

How hard could this be, anyways? I can weather this storm (can't I?). On that crazy boat trip for 11 days at sea, I was feeling a bit strange and nauseous from the onset. Oops I had forgotten the seasick pills! Captain Bob said it would only last 24 hours. I turned back nostalgically looking at the lights of Hong Kong. Suddenly, I had to puke. I was hanging over the side railing vomiting my lunch. It was going to be a long night. I had wondered if it was a bad omen? I won't spoil the story, but that adventure was no smooth ride without incidents. How could this be any worse? Thailand is a civilized country on dry land and I would find a legitimate way to survive. I do have a resume with English teaching experience and other unrelated, extraneous skills.

The other day I visited an Italian woman in jail because of her idiot boyfriend who manipulated her into carrying a suitcase with gold handles (she was convicted of smuggling gold). She will be there for 25 years minimum until the next King's amnesty---give or take a year. I could write a play, "The King and Her". At least I'm not exactly in jail? She looked pretty sad when I sat across from her in the caged visitor's area. I passed her some toiletries, but she only stared blankly out the window over my shoulder to the outside world (no real eye contact). After leaving the jail, I got to thinking. I've gotta look on the bright side; I can walk around Bangkok anytime, breakfast comes with my room, and dinner is freshly cooked---right in front of my eyes.

Gerrit just walked in. He's an artist from Holland living on and off in Nepal and Thailand for the past 20 years staying upstairs in a great spacious room with sunlight; the aroma of Thai weed drifts from the crack in the wall, so goes the rumor. He sits down to join me for 'dinner' (I think he feels sorry for me). Mama serves up our plates with a smile from ear to ear. Now she's my adopted mother, here in Bangkok. Gerrit splurges on a beer and pours me a glass. He tells me a story from his younger days travelling in India. He whispers, "You haven't really been in Asia until you go to India. Can't miss it." I say the same about China...he laughs. "You won't catch me in such a restrictive place." I try to explain a bit, then another backpacker comes by, and the conversation veers off to Chiang Mai in Northern Thailand. I retire early and say good night. I wink at Gerrit, "Thanks for the beer".

I am trying to finish my letter to Joan before sleeping. I learned tons from her, but now I am on my own at this point; my destiny is open and it's all about my own karma. I still miss Joan. She continues to be my cheerleader encouraging me to save up for the next leg of my journey around the globe. I must admit, no one back home really understands my dream. Thank goodness for Joan!

(To be continued---Unfinished)

Rosalinda Ruiz Scarfuto, a native Californian, began her artistic career with ceramics and poetry. She has lived and traveled from Japan to Spain walking the land including the Himalayas and Kenyan bush. Her first trip around the world was a 5-year sojourn completed by the age of 27. Over the years she has continued studying ceramics adding photography, wood block printing, painting and jazz to her repertoire. Her prolonged stays in Asia fostered her Buddhist philosophy. Rosalinda is available for international workshops about the Forest Flaneur methodology she developed in her doctoral thesis including creative writing, painting, and mindfulness. She enjoys her organic garden and yoga in her free time.

A photographic memoir of *China Blue 1984* is available by special order on her website, (forestflaneur.com) that includes a selection of original photos in a large book format.

www.ingramcontent.com/pod-product-compliance
Lightning Source LLC
Chambersburg PA
CBHW040759150726
48196CB00033B/869/J